Nature and Needs of Individuals with Autism Spectrum Disorders and Other Severe Disabilities

Nature and Needs of Individuals with Autism Spectrum Disorders and Other Severe Disabilities

A Resource for Preparation Programs and Caregivers

Edited by
Manina Urgolo Huckvale and
Irene Van Riper

ROWMAN & LITTLEFIELD
Lanham • Boulder • New York • London

Published by Rowman & Littlefield
A wholly owned subsidiary of The Rowman & Littlefield Publishing Group, Inc.
4501 Forbes Boulevard, Suite 200, Lanham, Maryland 20706
www.rowman.com

Unit A, Whitacre Mews, 26-34 Stannary Street, London SE11 4AB

British Library Cataloguing in Publication Information Available

Library of Congress Cataloging-in-Publication Data

Names: Huckvale, Manina Urgolo, 1952- editor. | Van Riper, Irene, 1947- editor.
Title: Nature and needs of individuals with autism spectrum disorders and other severe disabilities : a
    resource for preparation programs and caregivers / edited by Manina Urgolo Huckvale and Irene
    Van Riper.
Description: Lanham, Maryland : Rowman & Littlefield, 2016. | Includes bibliographical references
    and index.
Identifiers: LCCN 2015040381 (print) | LCCN 2015046749 (ebook) | ISBN 9781475820508 (cloth :
    alk. paper) | ISBN 9781475820515 (pbk. : alk. paper) | ISBN 9781475820522 (electronic)
Subjects: LCSH: Autistic children—Education. | Autism in children. | Teachers of children with
    disabilities—Handbooks, manuals, etc.
Classification: LCC LC4717 .N37 2016 (print) | LCC LC4717 (ebook) | DDC 371.94—dc23
LC record available at http://lccn.loc.gov/2015040381

This book is dedicated to my husband, Syd, who provides me with love and support while I undertake projects that, hopefully, will enhance the lives of others. I am truly blessed.

My life also has been blessed by my parents, who still provide me with a loving foundation and support for my career. My children, Alex and Lesley, and their growing families, provide me with a special love that keeps me going. – M.U.H.

This book is dedicated to my husband, Joe, who has provided me with support throughout the twists and turns of my career. He now knows more about autism than he ever imagined. His never-ending encouragement has sustained me throughout this project. Thank you, my friend, and companion.

I also dedicate this book to the students with autism who allowed me to learn from them while in the role of their teacher. It has been a privilege to know and interact with these amazing individuals. – I.V.R.

Contents

Preface

Students with special needs were provided with educational opportunities only on a limited basis until the initial passage of Public Law 94-142, the Education for All Handicapped Children Act (EHA) in 1975. Updated several times and, most recently, in 2004, EHA is now known as the Individuals with Disabilities Education Act (IDEA) whose purpose is to provide a free, appropriate public education (FAPE) to all students with special needs in the least restrictive environment (LRE) and prepare them for further education, employment, and independent living.

While teacher preparation programs have been training special education teachers for decades, most programs focus on working with students who exhibit mild to moderate disabilities. Textbooks for these programs then concentrate on strategies for teaching students who demonstrate mild difficulties with learning, for example, dyslexia, attention deficit/hyperactivity disorder (ADHD), developmental delays, and behavioral disorders.

A 2014 Google search showed no texts or programs focusing solely on working with individuals with severe disabilities. Teachers are generally placed in classrooms with this population and left to fend for themselves.

Our experience as teacher educators has shown that, while many of our graduates get jobs in general education classrooms containing just a few students with individual education plans (IEPs), more and more often they are obtaining employment in self-contained classrooms or in private schools for students with more severe disabilities. Many of these students are on the lower end of the autism spectrum with concurrent physical, intellectual, and behavioral disabilities. Student teachers and alumni have approached university faculty members, asking for a program that is geared specifically toward working with individuals with autism spectrum disorders and concurrent severe disabilities.

Reflecting on our own curriculum to prepare special educators, and listening to the concerns of our students, we saw the demand for a specialized program to satisfy their needs. They would then be better able to serve their students. Weekly meetings over one semester entailed intense discussions surrounding the prevalence of autism diagnoses in our state (one in 49 in New Jersey, see AutismNJ.org, 2013). As teacher educators, we felt a responsibility to prepare teachers to work successfully with this population.

New Jersey already has several graduate programs; however, the focus is solely on applied behavioral analysis (ABA). We felt that ABA was just one method for working with individuals with autism, so we decided to include other instructional strategies and methodologies (Lovaas, TEACCH, and Floortime, to name a few) for working with students on the low end of the spectrum, as defined by the DSM-5th edition, and other severe concurrent disabilities.

Acknowledgments

The editors are grateful to the contributors for their collaborative spirit and for sharing their expertise in this book. This volume could not have been written without the resources of our departmental colleagues who shared their insights and pedagogy, continually adding to the understanding and education of individuals with autism spectrum disorders and concurrent severe disabilities (ASD/ SD).

We particularly want to acknowledge and express our appreciation to Joe Van Riper for his technical expertise and the hours he spent editing and formatting this work.

In addition, we acknowledge the teachers and caregivers who have dedicated themselves to working with individuals with ASD/ SD. We hope that this collection will support their endeavors.

Introduction

The special education members of the Education Department faculty discussed our students' needs, met with our colleagues in the Communication Disorders Department, and did our own research to determine exactly what should be included in a new concentration within our M.Ed. program. It was decided unanimously that this program was indeed necessary.

The course topics would remain basically the same as our curriculum for mild and moderate disabilities, but the content would focus specifically on autism spectrum disorders and other severe disabilities (ASD/SD). Some courses were revised and others were newly created to maintain this focus.

Each chapter in this book is based on a course in the program, and while some courses are similar to our special educator endorsement program, the focus is specific to ASD/SD with a broad array of functional skills similar to typically developing peers.

The editors hope you find this book valuable. It is meant to serve as a guide for those in higher education who want to establish a program focusing on ASD/SD. It is also meant to be a textbook for such a program. Parents, caregivers, and others working with students on the spectrum may find it valuable as a resource for working with this target population.

Chapter One

Nature and Needs

Irene Van Riper, Manina Urgolo Huckvale, and Alexandra Gitter

"Autism Awareness" has become part of our culture. Driving down any American road without seeing at least one puzzle piece ribbon is rare. The number of individuals touched by autism has skyrocketed since Leo Kanner first coined the term in 1943. Millions of dollars are being spent to fund autism research and treatment, and knowledge about the disorder grows daily. Yet, despite all this, parents struggle to know what to do when faced with raising a child with an autism spectrum disorder (ASD). Educators and professionals, charged with preparing these children for a place in today's world, often feel unprepared and ill equipped for the job.

The purpose of this chapter, and those that follow, is twofold. The first aim is to provide useful tools to support the growth of individuals with ASD and other SDs. The second is to discuss ways to overcome common obstacles to such growth. These tools and strategies are drawn from the latest research, years of personal and clinical experience, and the curriculum developed for William Paterson University's M.Ed. in special education with a concentration in ASD/SD.

This first chapter seeks to describe the nature and needs of individuals with ASD through books and articles about the subject. It will also take a look at this disorder through the eyes of individuals with ASD themselves. This may serve to better illustrate their needs, challenges, and experiences. Also, the effects of specific applications and instruction will be examined in an attempt to equip those working with individuals on the spectrum with the skills they need.

DEFINING AUTISM SPECTRUM DISORDERS

How can we tell if someone has an autism spectrum disorder? Physically, they appear to be much the same as anyone else. But that is where the similarity ends.

The details of ASD definitions vary depending on who is asking. Those in educational areas will use different definitions than others seeking a clinical definition. Furthermore, these definitions continue to change over time as more knowledge is injected into the conversation.

But the most common elements found in such definitions echo those described by Kanner in his seminal paper documenting the first cases of autism, "Autistic Disturbances of Affective Contact" in the journal *Nervous Child* (1943). Kanner pointed out the developmental nature of ASD as well as the apparent lack of social interaction and communication and repetitive/restricted behavior:

> The outstanding, "pathognomic," fundamental disorder is the children's inability to relate themselves in the ordinary way to people and situations from the beginning of life. . . . There is from the start an extreme autistic aloneness that, whenever possible, disregards, ignores, shuts out anything that comes to the child from the outside. . . . It is therefore highly significant that almost all mothers of our patients recalled their astonishment at the children's failure to assume at any time an anticipatory posture preparatory to being picked up. (p. 242)

Of the children involved in the study, Kanner noted that most of them were eventually able to speak, while a few remained verbally silent. Even so, the children who, over several years, developed speech were still unable to converse with others. They showed an ability to repeat phrases in an imitative manner but seemed unable to follow basic rules of grammar.

Kanner also observed a distinct aversion to change in any form. A child with autism seems to have an "anxiously obsessive desire for the maintenance of sameness," even though he or she may occasionally cause a disturbance that interrupts that sameness. In his studies, Kanner found that several of the children were upset at the sight of broken or incomplete objects. He posed the idea that this fear of change and lack of completeness may, in part, account for frequent repetitive motions and the shortage of spontaneous activity found in these children.

The definitions of ASD currently used by educators and professionals contain similar features to those described by Kanner. For example, the Individuals with Disabilities Education Act (IDEA; 2004) defines autism as:

> A developmental disability significantly affecting verbal and nonverbal communication and social interaction, generally evident before age three, that adversely affects a child's educational performance. Other characteristics often associated with autism are engagement in repetitive activities and stereotyped movements, resistance to environmental change or change in daily routines, and unusual responses to sensory experiences. The term does not apply if a child's educational performance is adversely affected because the child has an emotional disturbance.

Clinicians use more recent definitions to identify individuals with ASD. One comes from the *Diagnostic and Statistical Manual of Mental Disorders*, Fifth Edition (DSM-5 [or DSM-V]; American Psychiatric Association [APA], 2013). Another definition is from the *Classification of Mental and Behavioural Disorders: Clinical Descriptions and Diagnostic Guidelines* (ICD-10; World Health Organization, 1992).

These classification systems are mostly "yes/no" checklists of behaviors and symptoms to determine whether or not an individual fits the definition of a person with ASD. It is commonly viewed, however, that there is a spectrum of autism disorders with no two individuals demonstrating exactly the same symptoms.

There is a saying in the autism community, "If you've met one person with autism, then you've met one person with autism." For this reason some researchers and diagnosticians have suggested approaching ASD classifications over a variety of dimensions, such as communication, social deficits, repetitive/restricted behaviors, as well as associated dimensions such as IQ. Because individuals with ASD often have varying levels of strengths and weaknesses in a number of areas, such a system might better capture the diversity within this population, allowing more specific classification and support.

PREVALENCE OF AUTISM SPECTRUM DISORDERS

Although disagreement regarding the precise definition of ASD continues, there is little debate that the number of individuals identified as having ASD is growing rapidly. According to a report released by the Center for Disease Control and Prevention (Zablotsky, Black, Maener, et al., 2015), the prevalence rate of ASD in 2014 was estimated at one in 45 children. This represents a 56 percent increase from the annualized rate from 2011 through 2013. By contrast, the same 2014 data showed no significant increase in other developmental or intellectual disabilities.

This dramatic rise in rates mirrors the increase in numbers of diagnosed students currently seen in schools nationwide. Theories explaining this rapid growth range from increased awareness, to a broadening of criteria, to increases of various toxins in our environment. The message seems clear, however. There are more children with ASD who need services and specialized educational support than ever before. On top of that, there are increasing numbers of parents, educators, and professionals now needing help in their efforts to meet the needs of these children. (See the Resources and/or References sections at the end of each chapter for a sample of recommended works on ASD.)

The same CDC report pointed out that there were variations in the prevalence of ASD when grouped by gender, ethnicity, or geographic area. Males were four to five times more likely to be diagnosed with ASD than females. This ratio has remained relatively stable over time regardless of geographic areas or ethnic groups. As in previous reports, the overall prevalence of ASD, however, did vary by ethnicity.

When compared to African Americans and Hispanic Americans, Caucasian Americans were 30 percent more likely to receive an ASD diagnosis than African Americans. That figure jumped to 50 percent when compared to Hispanic Americans. African Americans were 10 percent more likely than Hispanic Americans to receive the diagnosis. Rates also varied by region, ranging from one in 175 children in Alabama to one in 45 children in New Jersey.

ETIOLOGY OF AUTISM SPECTRUM DISORDERS

The specific causes of ASD are still not fully understood, and there is much debate regarding a variety of theories. There is agreement, however, that, contrary to years of well-intentioned wisdom initially proposed by Kanner and later popularized by Bruno Bettelheim in 1967, ASD is not the result of "refrigerator mothering," a term used to indicate a lack of maternal warmth. Rather, it is now commonly accepted that ASD is neurodevelopmental in nature with strong genetic roots.

Recent technological advances, such as the use of functional magnetic resonance imaging (fMRI), have helped answer many questions regarding ASD. Each answer has led to further questions, and the findings are often very complex and sometimes contradictory. Trying to prove a single theory explaining the cause of ASD is difficult due to the diversity of the condition.

Neuroscience and Autism Spectrum Disorders

Researchers have found a variety of structural and functional neurobiological differences common to individuals with ASD. For example, studies have consistently found increased brain size in early stages of development (Aylward et al., 2002). Furthermore, certain areas of the brain in individuals with ASD have been found to be underdeveloped, such as the corpus callosum, which enables communication between the two hemispheres of the brain, while other areas may be overdeveloped, such as the fear and emotional center of the brain (Nordahl et al., 2012).

Some research has also focused on rates of connectivity between various brain systems. Results have indicated patterns of hypo- and hyper-connectivity (slower and faster processing speeds) between different regions of the brain for individuals with ASD. These neurodevelopmental differences have been shown to correspond with the characteristic strengths and weaknesses often displayed by individuals with ASD (Charman et al., 2011).

GENETICS AND AUTISM SPECTRUM DISORDERS

Depending on the definition used, twin studies have demonstrated that ASD has a heritability rate between 70 and 90 percent (Risch et al., 2014). The autism genome recently found (Szatmari et al., 2007) was identified as the "autism gene."

In addition, studies have identified numerous possible gene mutations that may be linked to ASD, including some hereditary mutations resulting from irregularities passed down from previous generations and some spontaneous mutations that arise either in the egg or sperm before fertilization or soon after in the fertilized egg. Genetics researchers face difficult challenges since no one mutation has been shown to explain more than 1 percent of cases, and none seem to be specific to ASD.

Often the genetic mutations shown to be associated with risk for ASD have also been associated with risk for other disorders such as epilepsy, attention deficit/hyperactivity disorder, and schizophrenia.

The origins of ASD are not, however, exclusively found in genes, so other factors must contribute to its occurrence as well. A number of studies have identified various potential environmental factors that, when combined with genetics, may relate to ASD. For example, Gardener, Spiegelman, and Buka (2011) conducted meta-analyses that revealed associations between ASD and such factors as: maternal infection during pregnancy, gestational diabetes, umbilical cord complications, and even some neonatal factors.

Exposure to environmental neurotoxins at critical developmental periods has also been suspected as a risk factor for ASD. This line of research has sparked a lot of controversy, but there appears to be some evidence that such exposure may contribute to some cases of ASD (Grandin & Panek, 2013).

FEATURES OF ASD

Communication

Challenges with communication are often considered a defining characteristic of ASD. According to the DSM-V, individuals with ASD are typically very slow to develop language skills (APA, 2013), and approximately 30 percent of individuals with ASD are considered "minimally verbal" or "nonverbal" (Anderson et al., 2007; Kasari, Brady, Lord & Tager-Flusberg, 2013). These individuals seldom, if ever, use words to communicate. Some may have ongoing difficulties with language throughout their lives, including unusual patterns of speech, difficulties with conversational speech, as well as deficits in nonverbal communication (Eyler, Pierce & Courchesne, 2012). Additionally, understanding idioms or abstract language and sarcasm can be substantially challenging for individuals with ASD (Wang, Lee, Sigman & Dapretto, 2006).

Pragmatics Activity

Individuals with ASD/SD have deficits in pragmatics. Due to their developmental delay in communication, they very often have trouble engaging in discourse. They have problems maintaining and initiating conversations, staying on topic, and bringing interesting information to the table. These individuals are not able to recognize cues from the environment, so they may not know where their personal space is or where to stand in relation to their conversational partner. They may feel frustration and interrupt when engaged in a conversation, or they may have difficulty acknowledging that they have understood the previous utterance. For example, many individuals who are typically developing will signal their conversational partner with a nod of the head when they have received an answer. Turn-taking is another discourse function that individuals with ASD/SD may not demonstrate with facility. The lack of the ability to give and take in a conversation may be due to a deficit in joint attention. Typically developing individuals who have never experienced this stilted pragmatic situation may not know how it feels to be lost when engaged in discourse. Following is an activity that has been used to help experience/illustrate this type of frustration:

- This exercise involves three participants. Each participant is assigned a "job," although they are not privy to the "jobs" of the other people in the group.

    –One participant must tell a story, perhaps what they did the evening before, or something that might be of interest.
    –One participant is told to keep interrupting the storyteller saying, "What? I don't understand!"
    –The third participant must observe what is happening during this activity.

- The participants give their feedback after they are engaged in this activity for a few minutes. Each participant reveals how it feels to not be understood. They discuss what it feels like to constantly interrupt and experience frustration with their conversational partner. The observer most often sums up this experience. The storytellers describe how they try to keep explaining their story in several alternate ways to help the listener understand.

Limitations in the ability to communicate can lead to further problems such as frustration, aggression, isolation, anxiety, and confusion (Fleischmann & Fleischmann, 2012). It is, therefore, critical that individuals with ASD be taught the basics of communication early in their development. A number of strategies and technologies have been established to help these individuals develop communication skills as well as to assist those who already have some basic verbal abilities.

Interventions focusing on developing speech and language skills typically rely on behavioral approaches such as applied behavior analysis, or ABA. This approach should be used when incorporating alternative communication methods such as sign language, visual representation systems like the Picture Exchange Communication System (PECS), and assistive communication technologies.

In this instance, teacher candidates create a communication device using visuals, such as icons, or objects tailored to the student they observe throughout the semester. One such device may look like a folder or notebook divided into sections concerned with daily living skills and schedules. Students with ASD learn to utilize these icons to communicate a want or need. Another device may look like a credit card with a schedule on it that the student with ASD can keep in their folder or wallet. It may be used discreetly for navigation from one class to another.

An alternate type of communication device and schedule may look like a key ring with 2 x 3–inch cards attached for ease of use and accessibility. The cards will have icons that express a need or want, and/or a visual schedule. These cards may be color-coded so the student will remember the purpose for each card and be able to utilize it with facility.

The communication devices are taught to the student explicitly with the use of modeling and repetition. These devices can be implemented for nonverbal students, as well as students with minimal capabilities. They are tailored to the individual student and are not cost prohibitive.

SOCIAL SKILLS

Social interactions are extremely difficult for some children with ASD. The skills that are usually lacking include a sense of "give and take" in a discussion; the awareness of social norms and the ability to apply these norms; problems with initiating, maintaining, or joining conversations; difficulty maintaining friendships; and poor conflict resolution (Bellini, Peters, Benner & Hopf, 2007; Walton & Ingersoll, 2013).

The difficulties in recognizing and expressing nonverbal communication also hinder successful social interactions for these individuals. Difficulties in executive functioning limit the ability to take another's perspective, often leading to the perception that those with ASD are lacking in empathy. Although the degree to which each individual may experience any specific social deficit varies, the impact is great for almost everyone with ASD.

Due to the essentially social nature of society, the effects of these social deficits for individuals with ASD are substantial and may result in isolation, loneliness, peer rejection, bullying, and a general lack of friendships and meaningful relationships (White & Roberson-Nay, 2009). Stephen Shore is an adult with ASD. He was diagnosed with autism at 18 months old and was nonverbal until around the age of five. In 2012, Mr. Shore wrote of his early social challenges:

> As a young child, making friends in elementary school was difficult. Sometimes, I had one or two friends, but the school seemed mostly full of bullies. . . . Additionally, the friends I had were all older—they were either my sister's friends or adults. Thinking back, they may not have really been true friends, but since they were nice to me and listened to what I had to say, I considered them friends. (2012: pp. 65–66)

Social deficits can also directly and indirectly impact academic performance and the ability to get and keep a job. In 2006, Jane Meyerding, an individual officially diagnosed with ASD at the time, wrote:

> Given how much interaction is required by most jobs, it can feel as if we are working two jobs simultaneously. We need to do our work, but we also must expend huge amounts of energy on generating and maintaining a social interface. That's why I have been working part-time most of my life: if I try to work a full-time job, I need to spend the rest of my waking hours recuperating. Literally. (2006: p. 250)

Although they do not develop naturally for most individuals with ASD, social skills can and should be taught early on and throughout development (White, Keonig & Scahill, 2007). There are many social skills interventions and systems of instruction currently available. They vary in type including: video modeling, developmental- or relationship-based, peer-mediated, behavioral, and structured (Bellini et al., 2007). However, the effectiveness of these strategies has been mostly established with individuals on the higher end of the autism spectrum. Only limited examinations of these techniques exist regarding individuals with ASD and intellectual disability or other co-occurring conditions (McConnell, 2002; Walton & Ingersoll, 2013).

SENSORY PROCESSING

The DSM-V criteria used in diagnosing ASD do not include sensory processing issues. However, individuals with ASD are often found to be very sensitive to various sights, sounds, smells, textures, and other environmental stimuli. Bright lights and loud noises can be extraordinarily disturbing to an individual with ASD. Often their pain sensitivity falls outside what most would generally consider appropriate, as well (Moore, 2014).

Sensory processing issues have been linked to a number of additional conditions commonly found in individuals with ASD, such as gastrointestinal and feeding problems, sleep disturbances, central auditory processing, and problems with motor coordination. Caregivers of individuals with ASD should be aware of the behavioral responses to sensory processing differences.

Such differences can easily lead to strong feelings of frustration and anger, anxiety and fear, often resulting in unusual or aggressive behavior (O'Donnell, Deitz, Kartin, Nalty & Dawson, 2012). In fact, problems with sensory processing have been identified as a likely explanation for the repetitive and restrictive behaviors that are characteristic of ASD (Boyd et al., 2010). When combined with the difficulties of trying to communicate in addition to a deficit in social skills, it is not surprising that individuals with ASD struggle to navigate their day-to-day worlds in a socially acceptable and expected manner.

Anxiety

Individuals with ASD have the same worries and fears as everyone else; however, the way they show their anxiety will be more intense. New experiences, unplanned activities, and job interviews all cause some level of anxiety. The first step is to recognize what causes us to be anxious and then decide how to manage it.

- Recognize that anxiety is a natural part of life. Find out what makes you anxious:

    –Changes in routine (fire drill)
    –Changes in the environment (moved furniture)
    –Unfamiliar social situations
    –Sensory activities
    –Fear of a particular situation/activity/object

- Use relaxation techniques:

    –Counting to ten
    –Run around the gym
    –Look at a favorite book
    –Go to a quiet area

- Use social stories or picture schedules to show what to expect in certain situations. Rehearse stressful situations.

http://raisingchildren.net, accessed 11/16/2015

A number of interventions have been used to address the sensory processing issues associated with ASD and ease the sensory challenges. Such strategies include sensory integration therapies, therapist-constructed play activities designed to challenge sensory processing, and motor-planning skills.

There are specific activities designed to improve an individual's ability to absorb sensory information using specialized equipment such as swings, therapy balls, inner tubes, trampolines, and climbing walls. Additionally, massage, swinging, brushing hair, and bouncing on a ball may help decrease arousal related to sensory sensitivity. The goal of these types of intervention is to improve behaviors associated with sensory processing issues.

ANXIETY

There are a number of frequently co-occurring mental health conditions for individuals with ASD. Most common among these are anxiety disorders including specific phobias, generalized anxiety disorder, separation anxiety disorder, obsessive-compulsive disorder, and social phobias (Hutton et al., 2008; White, Oswald, Ollendick & Scahill, 2009).

After reviewing the literature on anxiety disorders and autism from 1990 to 2008, White et al. (2009) noted that 42 to 55 percent of children with ASD also met criteria for at least one anxiety disorder. When an individual is experiencing anxiety, cognitive abilities become compromised, hindering the performance of difficult tasks and impeding learning (Maloney, Sattizahn & Beilock, 2014).

Coping Strategies

We all experience different levels of stress. How we manage it can be exhibited in a variety of ways. For individuals on the spectrum, managing stress can be daunting. Some coping behaviors, while functionally necessary, can be disruptive. The goal is to develop more functional and appropriate behaviors rather than try to eliminate them.

Common coping behaviors:

–Repetitive patterns
–Biting
–Stimulation (stimming, rocking, humming, echolalia)
–Self-isolation
–Avoidance or intense seeking of sensory stimuli

Coping skills:

–Get a clear understanding of the cause of the stressor
–Acknowledge the stress and what one can and cannot control
–Learn/develop strategies to control the situation and reduce stress
–Actively make changes to reduce stress

Example: Visualization is a strategy that can be practiced almost anywhere and is used when feeling anxious, angry, or stressed. Find a comfortable, quiet area. Close your eyes and think of a place or object that brings back fond memories (a sunny beach, a favorite book). Focus on this place or object while taking deep breaths and relaxing your muscles. Do this for a few minutes. Evaluate whether or not this strategy worked in reducing your stress levels.

COGNITIVE FUNCTIONING

As previously stated, ASD is neurodevelopmental in nature, so it should not be surprising that the thinking processes of individuals with ASD often differ from individuals in the general population, sometimes referred to as "neurotypicals." Some individuals with ASD have significant intellectual disabilities, while others do not.

Research has further demonstrated that challenges in daily living skills and social deficits are greater for individuals with ASD who also have an intellectual disability (Charman et al., 2010; Walton & Ingersoll, 2013). It is also common that individuals with ASD demonstrate significant strengths and weaknesses in particular areas of their cognitive functioning. For example, individuals with ASD have stronger visual abilities than verbal abilities (Charman et al., 2011).

EXECUTIVE FUNCTIONING

Considerable attention has been paid to one particular area of weakness for individuals with ASD: the area of executive functioning. Executive functioning refers to higher-order thinking skills that involve connecting past experiences to present actions. These include planning, flexibility, self-control, self-monitoring, perspective-taking, working memory, time management, multitasking, and sustained attention. These are all associated with the functions of the brain's prefrontal cortex (Welsh, Pennington & Groisser, 1991).

Problems in these skills have been consistently demonstrated in individuals with ASD. Challenges in executive functioning affect most areas of life. It is vital in interpersonal relationships, academic and vocational functioning, and living independently. Due to the organizational component in this area of the brain, poor executive functioning may have more of an impact on individuals with ASD in adolescence and adulthood (O'Hearn, Asato, Ordaz & Luna, 2008; Rosenthal et al., 2013). Research has also shown great flexibility in the brain with some individuals with ASD. Research has demonstrated that the prefrontal cortex of the brain can thicken and improve over time (Luna, Doll, Hegedus, Minshew & Sweeney, 2007).

A number of interventions have been used to support executive functioning development. Others are used to make accommodations for these deficits. Cognitive-behavioral strategies targeting specific executive functioning skills have been shown to be effective. One such strategy is Unstuck and On Target (Kenworthy et al., 2013), which focuses on flexibility, planning, and goal-setting, while additional interventions target the development of executive functioning with neurofeedback and technological approaches (Riccio & Gomes, 2013).

BEHAVIOR

Unusual behavior tends to be the most obvious feature of ASD, and often presents the greatest problems. Less obvious, however, are the many possible explanations for this behavior. Although behavioral characteristics are part of the diagnostic criteria for ASD, they are most often the effects of other challenges associated with ASD. Understanding the nature and effects of these characteristics is critical to being able to empathize with individuals with ASD, and vital to supporting them and dealing with challenging behaviors.

When identifying a problem behavior, the first question one should ask is, "Why is this individual engaging in this behavior?" Is he or she having difficulty with communication? Is this related to a lack of social skills? Perhaps this person is overwhelmed with sensation? Or, could the cognitive demands be overwhelming?

REPETITIVE/RESTRICTED BEHAVIORS

The presence of repetitive/restrictive behaviors is common to most definitions of ASD (APA, 2013; Leekam, Prior & Uljarevic, 2011).

Other names for these types of behaviors include "stereotyped" or "stimming" behaviors ("stims"). The reasoning behind these behaviors, however, is not usually mentioned. Many individuals with ASD say that these are efforts to reduce anxiety. Sean Barron, an adult diagnosed at the time with ASD, wrote:

> I was born with a pervasive fear that never seemed to diminish, so I spent most of my earliest years devising ways to lessen the unrelenting terror, if not get rid of the chronic dread completely. To that end, I tried to find ways to look at and take in the world that would make sense to me and be less overwhelming while at the same time, provide a measure of comfort, control, balance and security—all of which were missing from my life. Isolating and manipulating objects while tuning out people; fixating on repetitive motions; asking the same questions over and over; developing stereotypical movements, arbitrary rituals and rigid thinking; and focusing to an extreme degree on one item or event to the exclusion of everything else were among the ways I found some control and security while temporarily sidestepping fears. (Grandin & Barron, 2005: p. 59)

Additionally, individuals with ASD may engage in these types of behaviors when they are excited or happy; or, they may occur due to sensory processing issues (Boyd et al., 2010). Oftentimes, these types of behaviors (spinning, flapping, counting, tapping) appear odd and atypical. They can be distracting or bothersome to others, and, in extreme cases, may even be harmful to the individual.

Most of the time, however, engagement in stimming is a coping strategy, and until the individual learns alternate ones, this behavior may be his or her only coping strategy. For individuals with ASD who experience high levels of anxiety on a regular basis, experience sensory processing issues, and are likely to have a limited ability to self-regulate, the need for these coping strategies may outweigh their "inappropriateness."

RESOURCES

Understanding both the historical context and current state of knowledge regarding autism spectrum disorders is key to the development of competency in teaching and supporting these individuals. The following writings and films represent a sample of recommended works for further exploration on the background of ASD (for bibliographic information, see references):

SEMINAL WORKS

- Kanner's (1943) original paper describing the case histories of his 11 patients sharing a core set of symptoms associated with what was later to be known as "autism."
- Bettelheim's (1967) book, based on the prevalent psychoanalytic theory of the time, which popularized the notion that autism was the result of cold and distant mothering, also known as the "refrigerator mother."

DOCUMENTARY FILMS

- Silver and Drezner's (2011) well-researched documentary, *Loving Lampposts: Living Autistic*, explores the world of autism, including its history, current schools of thought, and personal experiences of families and individuals with ASD.
- Davenport and Sullivan's (2014) film, *Too Sane for This World*, chronicles the personal experiences of 12 individuals with ASD.
- The 2010 documentary, *Neurotypical: Normal Is a Cycle on a Washing Machine* (Larsen, Larsen & Larsen), provides in-depth interviews with individuals with ASD and their families and explores the challenges they face living among "normal" people.

WORKS BY INDIVIDUALS WITH ASD

- Grandin and Panek's (2013) book, *The Autistic Brain: Thinking across the Spectrum*, provides a thorough overview of the neurological and genetic research on ASD while incorporating Grandin's personal experiences as an individual with ASD.
- Shore's (2003) autobiography describes his own history and journey in parallel with the history and journey of ASD research and culture.
- Lipsky's (2011) *From Anxiety to Meltdown* is a book on anxiety and its behavioral manifestations in ASD that incorporates her personal experiences and good suggestions for working with individuals with ASD.
- Bascom's (2012) *Loud Hands: Autistic People, Speaking* is a compilation of essays by individuals with ASD that explores the history, current realities, and advocacy movement of ASD.
- A number of videos by Dr. Temple Grandin clearly and succinctly describe the issues experienced by individuals with ASD and the needs of these individuals. Some examples:

    –Temple Grandin Video 5: www.youtube.com/watch?v=phYPqTJIRmA
    –Temple Grandin TED Talk: The world needs all kind of minds: www.youtube.com/watch?v=fn_9f5x0f1Q&list=PLL3XF6P7–IyM_9HmCyaoUwp7Q6ds-EP2E
    –Dr. Temple Grandin, "The Autistic Brain: Thinking Across the Spectrum": www.youtube.com/watch?v=IA4tE3_2qmI

- Fleishman & Fleischmann's (2012) book, *Carly's Voice: Breaking through Autism*, is a personal account of living as a nonverbal individual with autism. For an example of Carly's typical experience, view:

    –Carly's Café—Experience Autism Through Carly's Eyes: www.youtube.com/watch?v=KmDGvquzn2k

- www.wrongplanet.net is a Web-based community for individuals with Asperger's syndrome and autism created by Alexander Plank, an individual with ASD. The site includes a variety of resources for individuals themselves, as well as family members and professionals.

SUMMARY

The diagnosis of autism is a difficult process because individuals on the spectrum have symptoms unique to each person. The disorder is neurodevelopmental by nature and generally presents as deficits in communication, social skills, and atypical behavior. There are two primary methods of diagnosing ASD: educational and medical. The two criteria differ mostly in the definitions used to assess individual deficits. No single cause is known, although most agree that it is a combination of genetic and environmental factors, with a prevalence affected by gender, race, and geographic location.

With shortcomings in their ability to communicate, grasp abstract concepts, and unusual or seemingly antisocial behavior, getting an education is as much a challenge for the student with ASD/SD as it is for the teacher. The following chapters will outline the strategies and tools available to teachers and families coping with the nature and needs of a child with autism.

REFERENCES

American Psychiatric Association. (2013). *Diagnostic and statistical manual of mental disorders* (5th ed.). Washington, DC: Author.

Anderson, D. K., Lord, C., Risi, S., DiLavore, P. S., Shulman, C., Thurm, A., & Pickles, A. (2007). Patterns of growth in verbal abilities among children with autism spectrum disorder. *Journal of Consulting and Clinical Psychology*, *75*(4), 594–604. doi: 10.1037/0022–006X.75.4.594.

Aylward, E. H., Minshew, N. J., Field, K., Sparks, B. F., & Singh, N. (2002). Effecs of age on brain volume and head circumference in autism. *Neurology*, *59*: 175–83.

Bascom, J. (2012). *Loud Hands: Autistic People, Speaking*. Washington, DC: Autistic Self-Advocacy Network.

Bellini, S., Peters, J. K., Benner, L., & Hopf, A. (2007). A meta-analysis of school-based social skills interventions for children with autism spectrum disorders. *Remedial and Special Education, 28*(3), 153–62. doi: 10.1177/0741932507028003040l.

Bettelheim, B. (1967). *The empty fortress: Infantile autism and the birth of the self*. New York: Free Press.

Boyd, B. A., Baranek, G. T., Sideris, J., Poe, M. D., Watson, L. R., Patten, E., & Miller, H. (2010). Sensory features and repetitive behaviors in children with autism and developmental delays. *Autism Research, 3*(2), 78–87. doi: 10.1002/aur.124.

Charman, T., Jones, C. R., Pickles, A., Simonoff, E., Baird, G., & Happe, F. (2011). Defining the cognitive phenotype of autism. *Brain Research, 1380*(1), 10–21. doi: 10.1016/j.brainres.2010.10.075.

Charman, T., Pickles, A., Simonoff, E., Chandler, S., Loucas, T., & Baird, G. (2010). IQ in children with autism spectrum disorders: Data from the Special Needs and Autism Project (SNAP). *Psychological Medicine, 41*(3), 619–27. doi: 10.1017/S0033291710000991.

Eyler, L. T., Pierce, K., & Courchesne, E. (2012). A failure of left temporal cortex to specialize for language is an early emerging and fundamental property of autism. *Brain, 135*(4), 949–60. doi: 10.1093/brain/awr364.

Fleischmann, A., & Fleischmann, C. (2012). *Carly's voice: Breaking through autism*. New York: Touchstone.

Gardener, H., Spiegelman, D., & Buka, S. L. (2011). Perinatal and neonatal risk factors for autism: A comprehensive meta-analysis. *Pediatrics, 128*(2), 1–12.

Gjevik, E., Eldevik, S., Fjæran-Granum, T., & Sponheim, E. (2011). Kiddie-SADS reveals high rates of DSM-IV disorders in children and adolescents with autism spectrum disorders. *Journal of Autism and Developmental Disorders, 41*(6), 761–69.

Grandin, T., & Barron, S. (2005). *Unwritten rules of social relationships: Decoding social mysteries through the unique perspectives of autism*. Arlington, TX: Future Horizons.

Grandin, T., & Panek, R. (2013). *The autistic brain: Thinking across the spectrum*. New York: Houghton Mifflin Harcourt.

Hutton, J., Goode, S., Murphy, M., Le Couteur, A., & Rutter, M. (2008). New-onset psychiatric disorders in individuals with autism. *Autism, 12*(4), 373–90. doi: 10.1177/1362361308091650.

Individuals with Disabilities Improvement Act of 2004, 20 U.S.C. 611–614 (2004) (reauthorization of the Individuals with Disabilities Act of 1990).

Kanner, L. (1943). Autistic disturbances of affective contact. *Nervous Child, 2*(3), 217–50.

Kasari, C., Brady, N., Lord, C., & Tager-Flusberg, H. (2013). Assessing the minimally verbal school-aged child with autism spectrum disorder. *Autism Research, 6*: 479–93. doi: 10.1002/aaur.1334.

Kenworthy, L., Anthony, L. G., Naiman, D. Q., Cannon, L., Wills, M. C., Luong-Tran, C., & Wallace, G. L. (2013). Randomized controlled effectiveness trial of executive function intervention for children on the autism spectrum. *Journal of Child Psychology and Psychiatry, 55*(4), 374–83. doi: 10.1111/jcpp.12161.

Leekam, S. R., Prior, M. R., & Uljarevic, M. (2011). Restricted and repetitive behaviors in autism spectrum disorders: A review of research in the last decade. *Psychological Bulletin, 137*(4), 562–93. doi: 10.1037/a0023341.

Lipsky, D. (2011). *From Anxiety to Meltdown: How Individuals on the Autism Spectrum Deal with Anxiety, Experience Meltdown, Manifest Tantrums, and How You Can Intervene Effectively.* London, UK: Jessica Kingsley Publishers.

Luna, B., Doll, S. K., Hegedus, S. J., Minshew, N. J., & Sweeney, J. A. (2007). Maturation of executive function in autism. *Biological Psychiatry, 61*(4), 474–81. doi: S0006-3223(06)00381-7.

Maloney, E. A., Sattizahn, J. R., & Beilock, S. L. (2014). Anxiety and cognition. *Wiley Interdisciplinary Reviews: Cognitive Science, 5*(4), 403–11. doi: 10.1002/wcs.1299.

McConnell, S. R. (2002). Interventions to facilitate social interaction for young children with autism: Review of available research and recommendations for educational intervention and future research. *Journal of Autism and Developmental Disorders, 32*(5), 351–72.

Meyerding, J. (2006). Coming out autistic at work. In D. Murray (Ed.), *Coming out Asperger: Diagnosis, disclosure, and self-confidence* (pp. 245–57). London, UK: Jessica Kingsley Publishers.

Moore, D. J. (2014). Acute pain experience in individuals with autism spectrum disorders: A review. *Autism, 1*(March 31). doi: 10.1177/1362361314527839.

Nordahl, C. W., Scholz, R., Yang, X., Buonocore, M. H., Simon, T., Rogers, S., & Amaral, D. G. (2012). Increased rate of amygdala growth in children aged 2 to 4 years with autism spectrum disorders: a longitudinal study. *Archives of General Psychiatry, 69*(1), 53–61. doi: 10.1001/archgenpsychiatry.2011.145.

O'Donnell, S., Deitz, J., Kartin, D., Nalty, T., & Dawson, G. (2012). Sensory processing, problem behavior, adaptive behavior, and cognition in preschool children with autism spectrum disorders. *American Journal of Occupational Therapy, 66*(5), 586–94. doi: 10.5014/ajot.2012.004168.

O'Hearn, K., Asato, M., Ordaz, S., & Luna, B. (2008). Neurodevelopment and executive function in autism. *Development and Psychopathology, 20*(2008), 1103–32. doi: 10.1017/S0954579408000527.

Riccio, C. A., & Gomes, H. (2013). Interventions for executive function deficits in children and adolescents. *Applied Neuropsychology: Child, 2*(2), 133–40. doi: 10.1080/21622965.2013.748383.

Risch, N., Hoffmann, T. J., Anderson, M., Croen, L. A., Grether, J. K., & Windham, G. C. (2014). Familial recurrence of autism spectrum disorder: Evaluating genetic and environmental contributions. *American Journal of Psychiatry, 171*(11). 1206–1213. doi:10.1176/appi.ajp.2014.13101359.

Rosenthal, M., Wallace, G., Lawson, R., Wills, M. C., Dixon, E., Yerys, B. E., & Kenworthy, L. (2013). Impairments in real-world executive function increase from childhood to adolescence in autism spectrum disorders. *Neuropsychology, 27*(1), 13–18. doi: 10.1037/a0031299.

Shore, S. M. (2012). Stephen Shore: Special-education professor and autism advocate. In T. Grandin (Ed.), *Different . . . not less* (pp. 43–72). Arlington, TX: Future Horizons, Inc.

Szatmari, P., Paterson, A. D., Zwaigenbaum, L., Roberts, W., Brian, J., Liu, X. Q., & Herbert, M. (2007). Mapping autism risk loci using genetic linkage and chromosomal rearrangements. *Nature Genetics, 39*(3), 319–28.

U.S. Department of Health and Human Services, Centers for Disease Control and Prevention. (2009). Prevalence of autism spectrum disorders—Autism and developmental disabilities monitoring network, 14 sites, United States, 2008. *Morbidity and Mortality Weekly Report, 61*(3), 1–19. Retrieved from http://www.cdc.gov/mmwr.

U.S. Department of Health and Human Services, Centers for Disease Control and Prevention. (2014). Prevalence of autism spectrum disorder among children aged 8 years—Autism and developmental disabilities monitoring network, 11 sites, United States, 2010. *Morbidity and Mortality Weekly Report, 63*(2), 1–21. Retrieved from http://www.cdc.gov/mmwr.

Walton, K., & Ingersoll, B. (2013). Improving social skills in adolescents and adults with autism and severe to profound intellectual disability: A review of the literature. *Journal of Autism & Developmental Disorders, 43*(3), 594–615. doi: 10.1007/s10803–012–1601–1.

Wang, A. T., Lee, S. S., Sigman, M., & Dapretto, M. (2006). Neural basis of irony comprehension in children with autism: the role of prosody and context. *Brain, 129*(4), 932–43. doi: 10.1093/brain/awl032.

Welsh, M. C., Pennington, B. F., & Groisser, D. B. (1991). A normative-developmental study of executive function: A window on prefrontal function in children. *Developmental Neuropsychology, 7*(2), 131–49. doi: 10.1080/87565649109540483.

White, S., Keonig, K., & Scahill, L. (2007). Social skills development in children with autism spectrum disorders: A review of the intervention research. *Journal of Autism and Developmental Disorders, 37*(10), 1858–68. doi: 10.1007/s10803–006–0320–x.

White, S., Oswald, D., Ollendick, T., & Scahill, L. (2009). Anxiety in children and adolescents with autism spectrum disorders. *Clinical Psychology Review, 29*(3), 216–29. doi:10.1016/j.cpr.2009.01.003.

White, S. W., & Roberson-Nay, R. (2009). Anxiety, social deficits, and loneliness in youth with autism spectrum disorders. *Journal of Autism and Developmental Disorders, 39*(7), 1006–13. doi: 10.1007/s108003–009–0713–8.

World Health Organization. (1992). The ICD-10 classification of mental and behavioural disorders: Clinical descriptions and diagnostic guidelines. Geneva, CH: Author.

Zablotsky, B., Black, L. I., Maener, M. J., Schieve, L. A., & Blumberg, S. J. (2015). Estimated prevalence of autism and other development disabilities following questionnaire changes in the 2014 National Health Interview Survey. *National Health Statistics Reports*. 87. Hyattsville, MD: National Center for Health Statistics.

Chapter Two

Curriculum and Methodologies for Students with ASD/SD

Irene Van Riper

In a radio broadcast on February 9, 1941, Winston Churchill concluded his speech with the famous words, "Give us the tools and we will finish the job." These same words are quite appropriate today regarding the job of educating students with autism and severe disabilities.

There is a desperate need for readily available, innovative curricular and instructional methodology for individuals with low-functioning autism and other significant developmental disabilities. The biggest problem is that there can be no "one size fits all" solution. Autism is a spectrum disorder, which implies that each individual with autism has a unique set of needs and characteristics (Webber & Scheuermann, 2008). The manifestations of these disabilities are as different as fingerprints. Caregivers and educators are challenged to come up with a "recipe," combining several instructional techniques, to satisfy each individual student's education plan.

There are various methods educators may draw upon to help their students with autism spectrum disorder (ASD) and other severe disabilities (SD). Teacher candidates who are enrolled in this course observe a student with ASD/SD in several instructional environments. Teachers of individuals with ASD/SD must observe their students in every school-based context to determine the level of ability the student demonstrates. How do they behave in various classrooms? What are the actions they exhibit in the cafeteria or the playground? Important clues as to which methods might work better than others may be found in these observations. The Individual Education Plan (IEP) should be read and consulted for in-depth information.

The focus of this chapter is on specialized teaching strategies, and how to put these strategies into effect. Students with complex needs such as ASD/SD require differentiation of instruction, especially if these disabilities negatively impact their learning. This means tailoring the lesson to the strengths and weaknesses of each individual student. A typical example can be found in Jan, a young man with low-functioning ASD.

By the time Jan was in middle school, he had spent six years in a self-contained classroom for individuals with ASD/SD. In each class, depending on the training of his teacher, he was either taught by scientifically measured required tasks or placed in a corner of the classroom with crayons and coloring sheets. A scientifically measured required task might be to count how often he looked his conversational partner in the eye (eye gaze).

Often, Jan's instruction was driven by the educational training and background knowledge of his teacher. Considering that there are not many published curricula for individuals with ASD, due to the spectrum and varied instructional requirements, teachers of these students may feel that they are not supported as well as they would like (Shyman, 2012).

PARTNERING WITH PARENTS

With the stress levels and challenges that accompany the responsibilities inherent in placing individuals with ASD in the general population classroom (inclusion), teachers should attempt to understand the needs of the family as well as the student (Webber & Scheuermann, 2008). Teachers should develop empathy for the parents in order to support the student both at home and at school.

Tension was brewing at a recent IEP meeting for a student with ASD! The parents, teachers, and school principal met to hear the parents' frustration over the goals and objectives written for the student. The parents were adamant that the student's needs were not being met. The parents requested that goals for verbal skills and the conventions of conversation were to be added to the educational plan. The teachers had written only instructional goals and objectives for this student.

The parents, who wanted their child to be successful in all areas of living, asked for social skills to be addressed. Intervention was deemed necessary, and the principal stepped in. She suggested that the teachers write a goal and several objectives targeting pragmatics. She also suggested that the speech-language pathologist come on board and include the student in the weekly social skills group. The teachers, parents, and principal left the meeting feeling validated and content with the new addition to the IEP.

Parents of individuals with ASD may not want to admit that their child has a disability. Often a parent is not ready to accept such a diagnosis (Webber & Scheuermann, 2008). One mother revealed that, when her child was much younger, she was in denial, refusing to accept that there were any problems with her daughter. After a friend suggested that perhaps the girl had ASD, the mother stopped speaking to her friend.

Later, after the diagnosis had finally been made, this parent went through many stages of turmoil and introspection before attaining acceptance. One day, years after this child's diagnosis, the mother dropped her off at her middle school. The student came into class distraught, sat under a table in the classroom, and cried.

After trying to console the child, the teacher called the mother to ask for suggestions, and to inform the parent of the student's mood. The mom responded: "She's having an autistic day! I'll just come get her!" This parent had accepted the diagnosis, after much emotional upheaval, and was willing to work with the school to facilitate her child's education. Collaborating with parents makes a difference in the life of the child and for the family (Scheuermann & Webber, 2002). Parents and teachers should exchange information about the child often, including an overall accounting of what the child is learning in the classroom environment, and the success that they are achieving. Parents should be sure that teachers are aware of any changes at home, any new medication or family dynamics.

It is important to understand what role the parents play in the student's life. These are people who need the support and collaboration of the community, especially from their child's teachers. Individuals with ASD/SD need consistent methods and strategies both at home and at school. Teachers should meet with parents to offer information regarding how they interact with the student in the classroom. Ideally, the parents would work toward using similar treatments at home.

METHODOLOGIES TO SUPPORT
SOCIAL-EMOTIONAL WELL-BEING

One method to facilitate behavior and support individuals with ASD/SD that can be used in any environment may be a "First, Then" chart. This can be a simple piece of cardboard with the words "First" and "Then" printed on it, and a blank square after each word. Pictures or icons can be attached to the squares to remind the student of common actions they should follow. After the word "First," there might be a picture or icon of a math addition problem to indicate it is time to work. A picture of a snack might come after the word "Then." With this, the child understands that first they must complete their math classwork, then they may have a snack. A timer may be used with this method to further underscore what the time limit will be for the classwork and the snack.

Parents can be taught how to use this tool to create a strong and consistent environment in the home. From their experience in the classroom, the student will understand the use of the tool and will be comfortable with it.

The use of timers is also important in the classroom. This strategy gives the student the boundaries needed to support a productive day of learning. The teacher tells the student that they will perform a task for five minutes, and then sets the timer. The student can see the timer and understands that, when the timer goes off, a new activity will follow. This is a concrete and literal method for defining parameters in the school day. Parents can use timers at home in the same manner. This prepares the child for a change in activity or environment. The timer facilitates the change with little or no anxiety.

Social Stories (Gray & Garand, 1993) are stories that can be written by teachers or parents to describe social situations in which the student needs guidance. Social stories are simple stories written in age-appropriate vocabulary. They include pictures that may be in the form of photographs or artwork created by the student or teacher. The story is usually written according to the seven types of sentences prescribed by Gray and Garand (1993). Social stories are

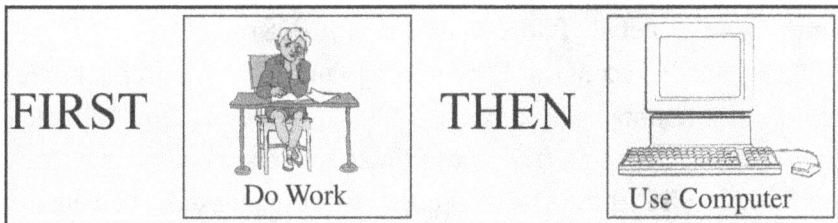

Figure 2.1. Typical "First, Then" chart. *Source: Layout: Van Riper, Art: Master Clips*

beneficial if read prior to the social situation so that the student is comfortable during the situation and knows what behavior is expected. Parents and teachers can share these stories for consistency at home and at school. An example of a social story, written according to Gray's requirements, is an important addition to any teacher's toolbox.

Teachers of individuals with ASD/SD must be familiar with a variety of evidence-based interventions so that they are able to offer consistent educational plans to their students. While many educational interventions are evidence-based, there are some strategies that do not have the research to demonstrate benefits for students with ASD (Shyman, 2012). According to Lord and Rissi (2000), ASD is defined as a "triad of deficits." The deficits involve social reciprocity, communication, and repetitive behavior. They also vary in degree and prevalence. These individuals are often delayed in language development and social interaction. Why must teachers use intentional and differentiated strategies to teach students with ASD/SD? The answer lies in the brain (Mason et al., 2008).

Brain activation in individuals with ASD is different than in their typically developing peers. Problem solving abilities that originate in the neural systems of the brain are usually a result of the integration of processing centers in the brain. Individuals with ASD utilize areas of the brain differently, and generally demonstrate strengths in areas involving visual processing. However, they often have difficulty with comprehension, perspective, and figurative language (Kana et al., 2006; Mason et al., 2008).

Consider this scenario. It's morning, and Bobby is in his homeroom class. Bobby gets anxious about his daily school schedule because he cannot find it. It doesn't matter if his schedule is written somewhere else in the classroom; he is not happy until he can see his own copy of the daily schedule. In a different setting, the words themselves may only add to his confusion. His unease will likely

MY TURN AT THE SWINGS

My name is Marcy. I am in the first grade. Sometimes I get angry on the playground.

The children in my class go to the playground to have fun and play on the swings. Sometimes other children get to swing before me. This makes me angry and I might push a child off the swing. That person could get hurt. I don't want to hurt anyone.

Sometimes I get to the swings first, and sometimes I may have to wait my turn to play on the swings.

Many children like to swing. The playground teacher knows who gets to the swings first. She knows about being fair and tries to let every child have a turn at the swings during recess time.

It is important to listen to the teacher. I know I will get my turn to play on the swings. It is okay to wait for my turn.

Figure 2.2.   An example of a Social Story. *Source: Layout: Van Riper, Art: Master Clips*

impede his learning. He may refuse to leave his classroom, exhibit fear, and cry or throw a tantrum. Bobby might crawl under his desk and scream that his "brain hurts." Without an understanding of how Bobby learns best, the teacher might feel frustration at lacking the tools to support him. Due to the fact that Bobby's strengths are visual, he needs to have access to his schedule, including any changes that might occur during the day. To support his autonomy and give him a sense of controlling his own life, he should be able to contribute his ideas and opinions when the schedule is first conceived.

If Bobby is in an inclusive setting, he may not have as much flexibility as he would have if he were in a more restricted classroom setting. Whichever placement a student is in, they should have access to and participation in creating their schedule.

For middle or high school students in an inclusive setting, their schedule should remain accessible, but discreet. It should be durable, portable, and easily accessible. It may be written on cardstock the size of a credit card to fit into the student's wallet, or it may be placed in a folder that can be peeked at easily from the student's book bag or three-ring binder. The mode chosen should be durable and transportable so the student will feel comfortable when the need arises to check their schedule. Sometimes students with ASD/SD require explicit teaching and practice using their specific type of schedule. If Bobby had a schedule such as one described, he would feel less anxious, and more like his typically developing peers.

For a student who may be in a special classroom or a self-contained situation, a schedule may be taped to a desk or put on a wall near the student's workspace. The student can learn to check off what has been accomplished, and will be able to see what tasks remain to be completed. For a student with ASD/SD who may need pictures to indicate daily events, small icons or photos can be adhered in place next to the text so the student sees the words and the picture. Given the opportunity to read the schedule and also be able to look at the picture of each event, the student will learn to recognize words related to the schedule, which will further decoding and comprehension skills.

PROCESSING ISSUES

Language processing in students with ASD is diminished due to the brain's weak central coherence that operates the linguistic and perceptual cues in speech and semantic processing (Jarvinen-Pasley, Pasley & Heaton, 2008). This means that individuals with ASD/SD lack the ability to infer meaning from social cues. A student with this type of challenge may act in an unconventional way. This is because they do not absorb the social cues from the environment, even after observing their peers.

In another scenario, Ella, an early teenager, just enrolled in a new school. She has ASD, but is placed in an inclusive setting with typically developing peers. She has the skills to move about independently in the school building and follows her teachers' instructions with relative ease. While sitting in her new homeroom, her teacher announces that it is now time for math class. Ella knows that math is in a different room with another teacher. The class must move to that new room. When her peers leave the homeroom, they all make a left turn and walk down the hall a short distance to the math classroom.

Ella leaves last but makes a right turn. She walks down the hall, out through the school's front door, and around the building. She enters the school through a back door and walks to the math class from the other side of the building.

No one has noticed that she takes a different route to the math class each day. She is always a few minutes late, and therefore she doesn't hear all of the math teacher's instructions. This causes her to become frustrated, and she puts her head down on the desk. To

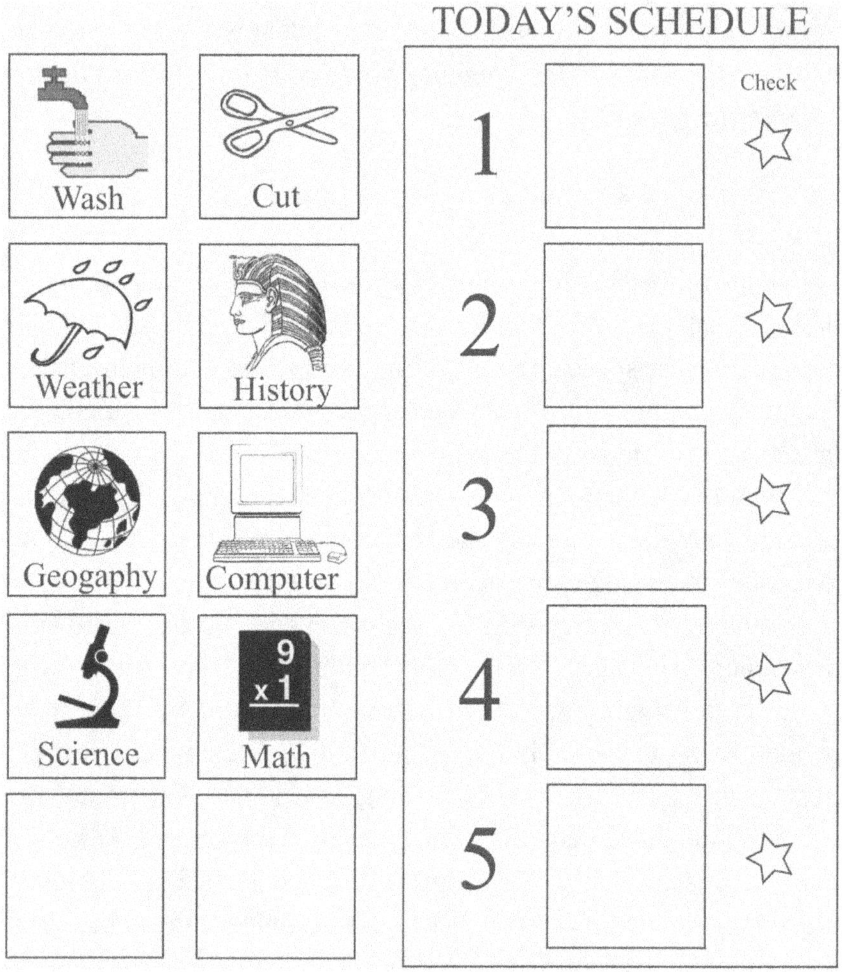

TODAY'S SCHEDULE

Figure 2.3.   One example of a visual support *Source: Layout: Van Riper, Art: Master Clips*

the teacher and other students, it appears as if she is disinterested. What could be done to support Ella?

The Power Card Strategy (Myles, Trautman & Schelvan, 2004) supports a student who needs guidance with understanding social situations, routines, and the hidden curriculum (p. 30). According to Myles, Trautman, and Schelvan (2004), the hidden curriculum refers to all of the tacit information typically developing individuals learn from cues in the environment. Individuals with ASD/SD may not have an understanding of these cues and may wonder why they don't have any friends, or why they feel like an outcast. The Power Card activity helps define some of the skills needed to feel more a part of the school community.

The power card is a portable, durable, and accessible communication device that a student with ASD/SD can learn to use to facilitate appropriate communicative competence. This strategy must be taught explicitly, and the student should have ample opportunity for practice. It is a two-part technique that calls for a "script" and the corresponding "power card."

The script, like a social story, is written in age-appropriate vocabulary. It is usually not written in the first person, however, substituting a familiar cartoon character or superhero, for example, that the student likes. The character is grappling with a social problem that the student may encounter, and offers solutions to the problem. The character gives the student advice on how to handle a social or emotional situation so that the student can relate it to himself.

The power card can be an index card or a wallet-sized piece of cardstock that states a brief summary of the steps for dealing with a situation that may prove to be difficult for the individual. The card can have colorful icons or pictures for visual cues to help the student remember how to solve a social or emotional problem. It should be laminated for durability and can be affixed to a folder or desk, or slipped into the student's wallet or purse for easy accessibility.

It is important for the teacher or caregiver to explain this technique with care and give the student many opportunities to practice using this method.

Information processing is hindered in individuals with ASD/SD by a deficit in Theory-of-Mind, or one's ability to understand another person's perceptions (Frith & Happe, 1999). When typically developing individuals reflect on how they think and learn, they are also able to understand how others think and learn. If that skill of metacognition is impaired, learning suffers.

Due to this type of deficit in information processing, the learner with ASD/SD may not be able to access prior knowledge appropriately. That individual then becomes overwhelmed (Frith, 2003). Educators and caregivers should be armed with the strategies and techniques for differentiating instruction that are needed to guide and support individuals with ASD. Goals and objectives, designed to enable that instruction, are important elements in the student's educational framework.

PRAGMATICS

Individuals with ASD/SD may have language acquisition delays, be nonverbal, or lack the understanding needed for competent communication skills. These skills may consist of initiating or maintaining a conversation, not interrupting, staying on topic, and demonstrating perceptual understanding of their conversational partner (Frith & Happe, 1999; Frith, 2003). So, an important goal for these individuals would be to engage in some type of appropriate communication. As a matter of fact, some individuals with higher-functioning ASD may not need educational goals but could still be lacking in the ability to maintain or initiate a conversation, as with the student mentioned earlier whose parents wanted to amend the IEP.

The inability to communicate efficiently and appropriately can be pervasive and get in the way of learning, along with impeding the individual's well-being and quality of life. Teachers might have the students engage in role-playing to practice conversational skills, or give two students a scenario and prompt them to discuss it. The phrases to be used could be written down for the students to read, or even displayed as small pictures or icons to help the conversation along. Students need to have these skills so they may communicate efficiently.

Feelings Cards are visual supports that facilitate communication. Individuals who cannot verbalize their frustration, anger, or anxiety may be taught to utilize these cards so that they can be productive and successful among typically developing peers.

For example, Jack is a middle school student with low-functioning ASD and is transitioning from a self-contained to a prevocational classroom. Jack is verbal and communicates well, but he has not learned how to express his fear or anxiety. He must be explicitly taught what to do to communicate his anxiety, fear, and anger when he has those feelings. He needs to have his teacher or caregiver help him understand the symptoms he might encounter that lead to feelings of anger or anxiety. So, his teacher or caregiver should discuss with him how he feels when he begins to feel anxious, and what he needs to do to control his feelings in order to remain in the inclusive setting. Jack was given these cards one at a time, and each feeling was discussed separately. He was taught that as each feeling arose, he should tell either the paraprofessional or the teacher that he needed to go out of the room, or to get a sip of water so that he could compose himself.

Before Jack had the cards and understood his feelings, he would get out of his seat in his prevocational classroom and shove the teacher. This aggressive behavior was his way of expressing his feelings of anxiety that impeded his learning. When he realized that he could express these fears to an adult, he was able to stay in the classroom and learn. Teachers or caregivers can use the cards in several ways. One is to support Jack's feelings so he knows how he should act in the situation. Another technique to implement the cards is to allow Jack to hold up a card to the teacher or paraprofessional to show what he is feeling, and allow him to "chill," leave the room, and come back ready to learn.

Each individual with ASD/SD has unique needs. Behavioral supports should be designed to uniquely meet those needs. For individuals with low-functioning ASD, there are several treatments that can be used and adapted, approaches that target behavior and emotional health to support educational needs.

Most students who are nonverbal can understand conversations and respond in their unique manner. A student of middle school age, who was nonverbal at the start of the school year, was given oral language in the form of a story about when he was a baby and how he grew up. The teacher told him the same story every day, with hand motions and tonal prosody to express the delight of his childhood and his growth into his teens. Since it was a story just about him, he was attentive to it. By the end of the school year, he was repeating the words and the hand movements. Along with his language development aligned with this particular story, he was acquiring new vocabulary and expressing himself verbally for the first time. His father called the teacher months later to report that his son came downstairs one morning and told his dad that he loved him! At the age of 12, this individual with ASD was learning and utilizing language through repetition and visual supports.

ANGRY   SAD   SCARED   HAPPY

Figure 2.4.   Graphics suitable for Feelings Cards. *Source: Layout: Van Riper, Art: Master Clips*

APPLIED BEHAVIOR ANALYSIS

Applied behavior analysis (ABA) is a research-based intervention that is comprised of several techniques to support appropriate behaviors for students with ASD and other disabilities (Alberto & Troutman, 2013). This technique can be used to increase acceptable behavior, and it has been used to enhance social skills and pragmatics. It may be used with Discrete Trial Training (DTT) that breaks skills down into smaller parts.

Each subskill is taught individually until mastery is achieved. After each skill is learned, the student might receive a reward, such as a sticker or a high-five. Software for DTT is especially successful for individuals with ASD because it is visually colorful, and progresses in skill level automatically, according to the mastery demonstrated.

PICTURE EXCHANGE SYSTEM

The Picture Exchange System (PECS) is a communication system that was introduced by Frost and Bondy (2002) in 1994. Individuals who are nonverbal find this communication system very appealing since they are generally most comfortable with interacting visually (Mirenda, 2001). Students are able to use pictures or icons to make requests, alleviating frustration with their verbal deficits. With the guided use of the PECS, individuals with communication delays or deficits can make requests and comments using these symbols. PECS also helps these individuals gather information to enrich their knowledge (Frost & Bondy, 2002).

SCERTS

The SCERTS model is used for enhancing communication and socio-emotional abilities (Dawson & Osterling, 1997). SCERTS stands for Social Communication, Emotional Regulation, and

Transactional Support. This approach is used in the natural class-room environment and is essentially a combination of methodologies for instruction and behavior. As with other objectives, the family is encouraged to collaborate with the teacher so that strategies for education and social skills are consistent in all environmental contexts, from classroom to home.

TEACCH

TEACCH, originally the Treatment and Education of Autistic and Related Communication Handicapped Children, is an approach that refers to ASD as a culture (Mesibov, Shea & Schopler, 2006). Although individuals with ASD/SD have a wide range of cognitive, social, and emotional levels, they respond well to structure. The learning characteristics of individuals with ASD/SD are addressed with the TEACCH approach utilizing visual supports for communication, organization, and autonomy. A TEACCH classroom is developed and constructed to embody structure and organization in the educational environment. The classroom is physically configured so that the student can enter the classroom the same way every day. The student knows exactly where to put his or her coat and belongings. They are taught to complete these tasks with explicit instruction.

After the students enter the classroom, visual and verbal supports prompt them to begin their day. TEACCH is a research-based intervention. A structured classroom might have desks that are separated by moveable walls so that the students can work on their individualized tasks without distraction. There is a "predictable sequence of activities" (Mesibov, Shea & Schopler, 2006: p. 41).

THE INDIVIDUAL EDUCATION PLAN

Every individual with a disability is entitled to a free and appropriate education, according to the Education for All Handicapped

Children Act of 1975. Since that time, reauthorizations of that act have contributed to the overall depth of education for individuals with disabilities. The Individuals with Disabilities Act (IDEA), another federal provision for individuals with disabilities, has gone through several iterations.

The most recent amendment of the IDEA was written in 2004. Within the scope of these federal acts, an individual education plan (IEP) is prescribed. The IEP is a legal document, and instructional best practices are detailed for the student (Parette & Peterson-Karlan, 2008). Both the parents and student are involved in the development of the IEP. Goals and objectives are written by the IEP team, which is a group of people comprised of professionals, parents, teachers, and sometimes the student. These goals and objectives spell out the instructional path the teachers and caregivers will take to best serve the educational needs of the student. For students like Jan and Ella with developmental disabilities such as ASD, the goals and objectives usually target functional instructional needs.

According to the IDEA, a functional need is one that allows for independence and quality of life (Parette & Peterson-Karlan, 2008). IEP goals are the overarching markers of the student's progress, and objectives are the steps with which students will achieve those goals. Teachers should be cognizant of the federal laws and what they state.

Creating an IEP is another assignment for teacher candidates who are in this type of course. It includes a narrative describing the student's present levels of performance (PLEP) with goals and objectives that are derived from the PLEP.

The IEP consists of a statement of the student's present levels of educational performance; a statement of measurable goals, including short-term objectives; as well as other components related to the educational program of the student. Educational goals are statements of instruction the student should master, actual instructional intent, for at least one grading or marking period. The goal should indicate the change of the target behavior, the deficit, the expected ending level or skill, and the resources needed to accomplish this change. Examples:

- Chad will increase his reading comprehension from primer level to first-grade reading level using one-on-one instruction.
- Jenny will increase her expressive language from speaking in two-word phrases to speaking in full sentences using a social group with the speech pathologist.

Short-term objectives are the steps to attaining the goal. They define the intended outcome of the instruction, they describe the level of performance, and they are easily understandable. Objectives must state the target behavior, conditions, criteria, and evaluation protocol. An intended time during the semester, or month, for the objective to be mastered may be included in the statement. Examples:

- By the end of the semester, Ann will identify five vowel sounds, after being given drill cards with icons, at 90 percent accuracy as measured by the teacher.
- Given 10 two-digit multiplication problems, Jeff will solve the math problems, with 80 percent accuracy as measured by an end-of-unit quiz.

The goals and objectives should relate to the student's level of performance, and be derived from the narrative describing that performance. The goals should match the unique needs of the student.

Teachers should become familiar with the procedure for writing goals and objectives, and be certain to include all of the essential components. If the student moves to a different instructional environment during the life of the annual IEP, the new teacher or caregiver should be able to continue the instruction with facility.

IDENTIFYING EVIDENCE-BASED
INSTRUCTIONAL PRACTICES

What is an evidence-based practice? When considering which instructional strategies to use for individuals with ASD/SD, the educator should study the student's cognitive and present levels of performance. Methodologies chosen should be based on the needs of the student. Evidence-based strategies are routinized and systematic (Spooner, Browder & Mims, 2011). These practices are offered in such a way that the student understands all of the instructions and knows what to expect. The instruction allows for the developmental growth and progress of the student at the unique rate most comfortable for them.

DIRECTED READING-THINKING ACTIVITY

The Directed Reading-Thinking Activity (DRTA) (Stauffer, 1969) is an evidence-based instructional practice that is routinized and systematic. It is a prescribed reading strategy that can be adapted for individuals with developmental disabilities like ASD. Van Riper (2010) adapted this instructional strategy for individuals with low-functioning ASD. Students knew in detail how each day's lesson would be presented. They were familiar with the educational vocabulary needed to hone their skills for reading comprehension. Vocabulary such as making predictions, summarizing, and visualizing were taught explicitly before the lessons began.

Each lesson was adapted for the students and followed their literacy goals and objectives. The teacher used a think-aloud method: a guided reading method in which the teacher stopped at various points in the story to describe what strategies were being used. For instance, if the group was reading the beginning of the story, the teacher might realize that the text was predicting what might happen later in the story. So, the teacher would state aloud what they were predicting or thinking. This type of explicit instruction is essential for individuals who have information processing deficits.

A physical modification for a student who might complain that the words are "running off the page" while trying to read, would be a pastel transparent overlay. This transparent overlay is placed over a page of text and has the effect of showing the words clearer. Students have reported that the pastel color "keeps the words on the page."

In this application, adapting the DRTA for the unique needs of individuals with ASD increased its effectiveness. Through discussion about what they read, the students were practicing pragmatics. Discussion was prompted every day by a question or series of questions provided by the teacher. Data was taken to ensure that progress was taking place and that skills were being generalized in other educational contexts (Van Riper, 2010). Common Core Standards for English Language Arts can easily be referenced with this activity. Reading comprehension, close reading, and analysis of the text are examples embedded in the Common Core Standards (Browder & Spooner, 2011).

An essential component of the DRTA is prediction. Students with ASD/SD may not understand the inferential meaning of predicting in reading comprehension. Predicting is taught explicitly to these students. They should understand that to predict means to guess that something may happen in a story depending on the immediate context clues. A prediction is not wrong or right; it is merely an educated guess of what we think may happen in a story. So, a comparison to the weatherperson on TV may be a good way to introduce this component of reading comprehension. The weatherperson looks at the radar and all of the weather maps and makes a prediction if there will be rain or snow or a sunny day. As the weatherperson, we gather all of the information we have read, and all of the prior knowledge we can brainstorm, and try to figure out what may happen. The prediction component of the DRTA lesson helps the instructor determine if the student is able to make predictions, and if not, support those deficient skills.

LITERACY METHODOLOGIES AND RESOURCES

There are alternative literacy materials that can be adapted and modified for students with ASD/SD that are aligned with the Common Core Standards. One such program is called "Bring the Classics to Life" by Edcon Publishing (2008). Many of these adapted books are written on a third-grade level. These books are published in a soft-cover format; however, for students who may have limited motor planning, it is better to put the pages of the book in a three-ring binder. The binder is easy to handle, the pages can be flipped easily, and the binder can be individualized for each student. The teacher might add graphic organizers and other tasks to the binder, so that all work is in the order it should be tackled. The organization of the pages helps make sense of the lessons for the individual who needs more structure and routine.

Reading A–Z (www.readinga-z.com), a resource for readers of all levels and ages, is a Web-based site where teachers and caregivers can select and create books. The books and stories can be downloaded and printed. They can be used in many different ways to target the needs of the individual student with ASD/SD.

News-2-You (www.n2y.com) is another literacy resource that is easily adapted to the student. News-2-You is a newspaper that is written in a combination of words and icons. They offer four reading levels, and are appealing to students because of the formatting of the text. With each edition, the student can read current events, sports, recipes, jokes, and activities tailored to the current events featured in that edition. The newspaper also reinforces the vocabulary found in the stories by including attractive games and puzzles to ensure mastery of learning.

Name _____ Date _____

Title _____ Author _____

Key: R=Rarely; S=Sometimes; U=Usually; NO=Not Observed

BEFORE READING

___ Uses title and cover as support.

___ Uses knowledge of how stories work.

___ Uses own experiences.

___ Can select text that supports predictions.

___ Can differentiate between predictions based on text and predictions based on personal experiences.

___ Understands that predictions can be off target at this point.

DURING READING

___ Uses the story to support predictions.

___ Predicts more logically as more of the story is read.

___ Uses predictions to continue to create a need to read on and find out.

AFTER READING

___ Rereads to adjust predictions.

___ Uses story to support adjustments.

___ Confirms those predictions that were on target.

Strengths: Needs:

Student's Comments:

Negotiated Goal(s):

Figure 2.5. DRTA prediction checklist. *Source: Irene Van Riper*

Another evidence-based program is The Reading Comprehension Kit for Hyperlexia and Autism (www.linguisystems.com). It can be individualized and self-paced depending on the reading level and instructional needs of the student. Vocabulary, story grammar, summarizing, and questioning are targeted skills. In one middle school classroom for low-functioning students with ASD/SD, the teacher read the stories to the students using the think-aloud technique. Although the stories chosen were on a first-grade reading level, they did appeal to the middle school students as they were embedded with interesting factual material, and illustrations that expressed feelings and body language. Activities to access prior knowledge and brainstorming were used with these stories, as well as cloze sentences that provided guidance to respond to questions pertaining to the stories.

Edmark (www.proedinc.com) is a research-based reading program that was developed in the 1960s. This program is suited to students with ASD/SD because it offers instruction in several attainable steps. The program can be modified and individualized to the unique instructional needs of individuals with reading and comprehension deficits.

Universal Design for Learning (Rose & Meyer, 2002) is an instructional framework that allows for students to learn and express mastery of learning through different networks. It is a brain-based program that is built on brain and learning research (www.cast. org). The Cast.org website can be used to support students with ASD/SD as it offers technological guidance for reading comprehension and decoding. Students can use the speech-to-text format so that the text is read to them. Holograms from the Thinking Reader section of the website explain various strategies essential for reading success and are appealing to students who would benefit from the extra verbal and visual guidance.

An evidence-based math strategy for students with ASD is Touch Math (www.touchmath.com). Students with ASD/SD need multisensory instruction that strengthens the neural activity in the brain. Touch Math is a program that is visual and tactile. Each numeral has a touch point that helps the student remember the number value and can be used for teaching addition, subtraction, multiplication, and division. It can be used as a remedial program for individuals who need specialized and individualized instruction. To add to the kinesthetic and sensory needs of one student with ASD, a slant board was introduced to write on. This inclined board strengthened motor skills and pencil grip. Sandpaper was put under a sheet of plastic that was adhered to the slant board to help as a sensory advantage.

The physically structured classroom will also have a structured educational system. The "morning meeting" is a time when all students in the class gather to discuss the day. The calendar is presented and all students are encouraged to repeat the day of the week and the date. Weather is discussed as each student looks out the window and tells either verbally or with a picture what they deem is the weather for the day. Weather vocabulary is introduced and used to describe what is seen. A student with ASD/SD may have a special interest in the weather and can be deemed the "weatherperson" for the class. The daily schedule, which is laid out on the board, is discussed in detail. The teacher, caregiver, or student may have the responsibility of filling in the schedule. Any changes in the routine are discussed at this time so that there are fewer anxious moments due to an unanticipated change. If there will be a new activity during the day, it is discussed to allay any fears. A photograph or icon of each activity or setting can be added to the schedule so the student is comfortable as the day progresses.

If there is a community-based trip designated for that day, students should be aware of the destination and what they will be expected to do when they reach that destination. A middle school or high school class may go on weekly community-based trips to learn how to navigate in public settings. Students may want to be familiar with the building and whom they will meet. Photographs of what they will see and people they may encounter will help alleviate any anxiety. A brief discussion of the expectations and parameters for the trip will be helpful.

Students with lower cognition of all ages can learn, with guidance, to count the days in the calendar and repeat the day of the week. Every student should be encouraged to participate in the morning meeting. They might explain what they did on the weekend or the past evening. They may want to just state the day of the week, or the month. They may tell what activity they are excited about completing. The teacher may prompt the student by asking questions that cue the answer. For example, the teacher might ask, "Which activity that we just discussed from our schedule would you like to do today?" The student should be encouraged to answer in a complete sentence. Giving appropriate language to students with ASD/SD benefits language acquisition and competency.

DAILY LIVING SKILLS

Daily living skills are essential in everyone's life. Individuals with ASD/SD may need explicit help to support their daily needs. One middle school teacher of individuals with ASD reached out to the community and invited the local culinary school to come to her classroom to teach her students how to make pizza or cookies. The culinary school sent would-be chefs who wanted to help. They brought chef's hats and aprons for the middle school students and worked alongside these students as they made a variety of delicacies!

Students with ASD/SD will benefit greatly from interaction with their typically developing peers. They may be assigned a peer buddy to help them through an activity, or to sit with them in the school cafeteria as they enjoy lunch and conversation.

In one middle school, some students with ASD/SD participated in the school by learning how to use the school washing machine and dryer, doing laundry for the cafeteria or lost and found. One secretary in the middle school was so excited about the skills the students learned, she brought some of her laundry from home for the students to do. They felt productive and useful while learning a new skill essential to their lives. There are many ways to incorporate daily living skills into the classroom curriculum to aid and support students with ASD/SD.

SUMMARY

Students with ASD/SD exhibit their deficiencies differently from each other and therefore require differentiated instruction in order to be successful in school. The details of how this should be achieved are found in the IEP that is designed for each individual diagnosed with ASD/SD, and is to be followed closely by the student's teacher(s). Parental participation is also critical to the student's success.

Many strategies exist that have proven effective in teaching students with ASD/SD, such as the "First, Then" Chart, Social Stories, and a variety of visual supports like Power Cards and Feelings Cards. Complications in communication arise from the inability of these students to understand another person's perspective, and their lack of recognition and understanding of the social cues vital to the art of discussion.

We must always remember that individuals with ASD/SD are not necessarily lacking intelligence. They are often only lacking communication skills. If we recognize that this generation of students with ASD/SD represents a vast untapped resource for human society, it is easy to see the importance of educating these individuals as they grow into adulthood. It's a matter of devising the innovative curricular and instructional methodologies that will reach people who learn differently. We must give them the tools with which they can make better lives for themselves as well as for the rest of society.

REFERENCES

Alberto, P. A., & Troutman, A. C. (2013). *Applied behavior analysis for teachers* (9th ed.). Upper Saddle River, NJ: Pearson.

Browder, D. M., & Spooner, F. (2011). *Teaching students with moderate and severe disabilities.* New York: Guilford Press. Bring the classics to life. (2008). New York: Edcon Publishing.

Dawson, G., & Osterling, J. (1997). Early intervention in autism: Effectiveness and common elements of current approaches. In Guralnick (Ed.), *The effectiveness of early intervention: Second generation research* (pp. 307–26). Baltimore: Brookes.

Frith, U. (2003). *Autism: Explaining the enigma* (2nd ed.). Malden, MA: Blackwell Publishing.

Frith, U., & Happe, F. (1999). Theory of mind and self-consciousness: What is it like to be autistic? *Mind and Language, 14*(1), 1–22.

Frost, L. A., & Bondy, A. S. (2002). *The picture exchange communication system training manual* (2nd ed.). Newark, DE: Pyramid Educational Products, Inc.

Gray, C., & Garand, J. D. (1993). Social stories: Improving responses of students with autism with accurate social information. *Focus on Autistic Behavior, 8*(1), 1–10.

Jarvinen-Pasley, A., Pasley, J., & Heaton, P. (2008). Is the linguistic content of speech less salient than its perceptual features in autism? *Journal of Autism and Developmental Disorders, 38*: 239–48.

Kana, R. K., Keller, T. A., Cherkassy, V. L., Minshew, N. J., & Just, M. A. (2006). Sentence comprehension in autism: Thinking in pictures with decreased functional connectivity. *Brain, 129*(9), 2484–93.

Lord, C., & Rissi, S. (2000). Diagnosis of autism spectrum disorders in young children. In A. M. Wetherby & B. M. Prizant (Eds.), *Autism spectrum disorders: A transactional developmental perspective* (Volume 9, pp. 11–30). Baltimore: Paul H. Brookes Publishing Co.

Mason, R., Williams, D. L., Kana, R. K., Minshew, N., & Just, M. A. (2008). Theory of mind disruption and recruitment of the right hemisphere during narrative comprehension in autism. *Neuropsychology, 9*(2), 255–61.

Mesibov, G. B., Shea, V., & Schopler, E. (2006). *The TEACCH approach to autism spectrum disorders.* New York: Springer.

Mirenda, P. (2001). Austism, argumentative communication, and assistive technology: What do we really know? *Focus on Autism and other Development Disabilities 16*(3), 141–51.

Myles, B. S., Trautman, M. L., & Schelvan, R. L. (2004). *The hidden curriculum: Practical solutions for understanding unstated rules in social situations.* Shawnee Mission, KS: Autism Asperger Publishing Co.

Parette, H. P., & Peterson-Karlan, G. R. (2008). *Research-based practices in developmental disabilities* (2nd ed.). Austin: Pro-ed.

Rose D. H., & Meyer, A. (2002). *Teaching every student in the digital age: Universal design for learning.* Alexandria, VA: Association for Supervision and Curriculum Development.

Scheuermann, B., & Webber, J. (2002). *Autism: Teaching DOES make a difference.* Belmont, CA: Wadsworth-Thomson Learning.

Shyman, E. (2012). Education in autism spectrum disorders: A potential blueprint. *Education in Autism and Developmental Disabilities, 47*(2), 187–97.

Spooner, F., Browder, D. M., & Mims, P. (2011a). Evidence-based practices. In D. M. Browder & F. Spooner (Eds.), *Teaching students with moderate and severe disabilities* (pp. 92–125). New York: Guilford Press.

Stauffer, R. G. (1969). *Directing reading maturity as a cognitive process.* New York: Harper and Row.

Van Riper, I. (2010). The effects of the directed-reading thinking activity on reading comprehension skills of middle school students with autism. Unpublished doctoral dissertation, Widener University, Chester, PA.

Webber, J., & Scheuermann, B. (2008). *Educating students with autism: A quick start manual.* Austin: Pro-ed.

Chapter Three

Assessment for Students with ASD/SD

Michelle Gonzalez and Carol Maniscalco

The primary purpose of assessment is to obtain and gather information relevant to students in order to identify both their strengths and needs. The gathered information is used to facilitate effective decision-making with regard to the students we instruct. This chapter begins with the presentation of two case studies that illustrate the positive outcomes of assessment. The chapter includes a discussion of key terminology in assessment. The screening, diagnostic, and evaluation processes of autism spectrum disorders (ASD) are also examined. The chapter concludes with a discussion of classroom assessments. Though this chapter primarily focuses on ASD, many of the concepts discussed can be applied to other severe disabilities.

THE CASE OF MAURICE

Maurice was thought to be on the autism spectrum throughout his entire life in elementary school, and spent most of his time in school coloring with crayons and having no real academic demands placed on him. Then, one day during lunch with his classmates in his self-contained classroom for students with autism, his teacher casually asked, "How was your lunch, Maurice?"

The 12-year-old boy answered, "Great! It really hit the spot."

His teacher was surprised and became very curious!

Why? Because one of the symptoms of autism is an inability to understand and articulate idioms, or deal with abstract thought. If you tell a boy with autism that something "hit the spot," he will want to know which spot, what spot, where's the spot, etc. Someone with autism will take those words quite literally. If something "hit the spot," that means it must have actually struck a literal spot, somewhere! This was not a comment likely to come from someone on the spectrum.

As a result of Maurice's offhanded remark that his lunch "hit the spot," the teacher requested a reevaluation of his classification, which resulted in the discovery that Maurice was, in fact, not on the autism spectrum at all but was classified as having an intellectual disability. The behaviors he demonstrated were learned from years of being immersed in a self-contained classroom for children with autism. The ensuing adjustments to his IEP put Maurice on a new plan with which he began to blossom and flourish as a student.

THE CASE OF CARMEN

Carmen was diagnosed with autism as a toddler. When Carmen was 24 months old, his parents began to have some concerns about his development. He was not doing many things that his brother did at that age, and his behavior differed dramatically from many of the children in his playgroup. Carmen preferred to play alone and appeared not to enjoy interacting with his parents or his older brother. His parents remarked that he had trouble with communication. He had words but could not use them to communicate, and sometimes, when he got excited, he would display hand flapping.

There were instances, too, when Carmen would throw tantrums and repeatedly bang his head on the floor, often leading to an egg-sized lump on his head. He would also scream and throw a tantrum when he heard loud noises, such as the toilet flushing or a blender running. Carmen's parents brought their concerns to his pediatrician, who noted that his behavior traits were consistent with the characteristics of ASD. The pediatrician suggested that Carmen's parents complete a screening tool for autism. The results of the screening tool indicated that Carmen was at "High Risk" for autism.

The pediatrician recommended that Carmen's parents pursue further evaluation to determine if, in fact, he did have autism, and that Carmen see a developmental pediatrician with an expertise in autism.

Carmen was evaluated using specific tests geared toward the diagnosis of autism. These tests included parent interviews and observations. Other professionals, such as a speech therapist, occupational therapist, and physical therapist, also evaluated Carmen. After the multidisciplinary evaluation, Carmen was indeed deemed to have autism. His parents felt some relief at getting a diagnosis, but at the same time they were overwhelmed and scared, knowing that autism is "forever."

Carmen began getting early intervention services in his home. When he transitioned to preschool and elementary school, Carmen received high-quality instruction that gave him access to the general education curriculum. Appropriate strategies, accommodations, and modifications were put in place to ensure his success in the classroom.

Over time, Carmen's autistic behaviors changed or altered. He could communicate with his family, peers, and teachers. Many of his self-injurious behaviors diminished. Carmen still had difficulty making friends and demonstrating appropriate behavior, but his special education teacher was working with him on these social skills. Carmen's parents were thrilled with his progress. They attributed his success to his early diagnosis, the early intervention services he received, and the high-quality education given in the local elementary school.

USING ASSESSMENT RESULTS

The stories of Maurice and Carmen are only two of many possible positive outcomes that assessments may yield in the classroom. The information garnered from an assessment can be utilized for a variety of purposes including:

- Screening: The process of collecting data to determine whether or not additional assessments are needed to correctly classify students (Spinelli, 2012). We screen students to diagnose problems, to identify areas of strengths as well as areas that need support, and to ensure proper educational placement.
- Diagnosis: The identification of a disorder like autism. Most often a medical professional using the criteria found in the *Diagnostic and Statistical Manual of Mental Disorders*, Fifth Edition (DSM-V; APA 2013) makes a diagnosis.
- Eligibility: The decision that the multidisciplinary team makes to determine if the student is eligible for classification or special education services. Eligibility is determined from the interpretation of information gathered through the evaluation process.
- Instructional planning: Child Study Teams (CST) or Multidisciplinary Teams (MDT) and the individual education plan (IEP) placement team utilize assessment information to ensure the IEP is in accordance with the goals and objectives necessary for that student to benefit from the planned instruction. Educational goals are established that reflect the results of the assessments. These goals build upon the educational strengths of the student and, through the use of short-term objectives, assist educational specialists in moving the student forward toward age- , grade- , and socially appropriate goals.
- Progress status: The use of assessment data by educational specialists to continually assess the student during instruction. This data is periodically reviewed to determine the effectiveness of

the current program, and to justify when any adjustments in that program need to be made.

- Progress monitoring: The continuous monitoring of students' progress by teachers, analysis of the results, and the use of these results to implement any additional modifications or accommodations the student needs to attain instructional success. Continual progress monitoring is an integral part of the classroom assessment environment.

ASSESSMENT TERMINOLOGY

Before exploring key concepts of assessment and ASD, it is essential to discuss assessment terminology. Knowing assessment vocabulary will allow you to gain a better understanding of the assessment process and the interpretation of assessment results. In reference to the ASD/SD student, the vocabulary of assessment can be confusing. Words such as "standardized," "criterion-referenced," "validity," and "reliability" apply to all assessments.

Terms such as "assessment of program effectiveness," "progress reporting," "evidence-based practices," and "observational assessment" apply to the day-to-day classroom environment. Before you can understand the assessments relevant to the classroom, you must understand the vocabulary relevant to all assessments.

The term "standardized" is a term frequently used with assessment instruments. "Standardized" is defined as objective assessments. Most often they are created in a multiple-choice format. They were developed to assist in providing broad indicators of a student's performance within a selected area (Spinelli, 2012). In other words, standardized assessments compare a student's performance to that of age- and grade-level peers. Additionally, they are standardized in relation to the timing and scripting utilized by the proctor.

Standardized assessments can be categorized as one of two types: a formal standardized assessment, or an informal or nonstandardized assessment. An informal or nonstandardized assessment is frequently used in the classroom. This can be in the form of a curriculum- or performance-based assessment. The instructor may use the results to advance current instruction or to remediate where needed.

A "criterion-referenced" assessment is a test or other type of assessment that provides a measure of the student's performance (Jennings, Caldwell, & Lerner, 2006). The results can be utilized to design instructional tasks for students. The goal of the assessment is to define the specific knowledge and skills demonstrated by the student. A criterion-referenced assessment is usually scored using checklists, rating scales, raw scores, or percentages. They are usually user-friendly and can be administered by both teachers and paraprofessionals.

Two terms that are often used when discussing assessments are "validity" and "reliability." "Validity" refers to the degree to which the test actually measures what it claims to measure (ysu.edu, 2015). An example of this would be asking a job applicant to place round and square pegs in corresponding holes within a given time limit. Would this be a valid assessment of job performance? Only if the job required the applicant to place round and square pegs in corresponding holes within given time limits!

"Reliability" refers to the degree to which a test is consistent and stable in measuring what it is intended to measure (ysu.edu, 2015). Most simply put, a test is reliable if it is consistent within itself and across time. To understand reliability, consider two classroom teachers assessing their students' phonics skills. One teacher reads the word list (*boat, ball, bat*, etc.) and asks her students to indicate the initial sound they heard. The other teacher reads the same words, but stresses the initial consonant (*bbbboat, bbbball, bbbbat*, etc.).

The results from the second teacher's assessment would not be reliable. The students were prompted to recognize the correct response by the teacher's over-enunciation of the "B" sound, rather than by their own phonics skills. This compromised the accuracy of the test.

The remaining two terms associated with assessment are "formative" and "summative." These are probably the two most important terms utilized by instructors. Classroom instructors continually assess their students through these measures.

"Formative" assessments are ongoing and are used by the instructor to regularly monitor students' learning progress throughout the instructional period. By using formative assessments, the instructor can continually adjust his instruction to meet the students' learning needs. Some formative assessment strategies include having the students write in journals or on index cards what their individual understanding of a topic is. They may be asked to create exit cards that condense the learning into one or two simple statements.

Another strategy is the use of "bell ringers" or "pair and shares," where students share their knowledge with peers. Classroom teachers also use "thumbs up/thumbs down" as simple forms of exhibiting students' understanding of the concepts. Instructors, depending on the formative assessment results, can provide accelerated instruction or remediation to the students they serve.

"Summative" assessments are simply what the name implies. They are, essentially, report cards. They assess the sum of a student's performance. Summative assessments are usually administered by the instructor and appear in the form of chapter tests, benchmark assessments, midterm and final exams. The results of summative assessments usually become the basis for averages or grades. Since they are the "sum" of instruction, the instructor rarely utilizes these results to adjust the instruction (Spinelli, 2012).

Comprehending the previously discussed terminology will lead to a better understanding of the processes and assessments used in screening, diagnosis, and eligibility classroom assessment.

SCREENING

The Steps of the Screening Process

Often the first step in the assessment process of identifying a child with autism is screening. The purpose of screening in the assessment process is to determine if further evaluation is needed. The use of screening is key because it can lead to early identification of ASD. The sooner a child is diagnosed with ASD or is suspected of having ASD, the sooner the child can benefit from early intervention services.

Children who receive early intervention services are more likely to have better outcomes (Boyd & Shaw, 2010) than those children who do not. Also, early intervention started prior to age three and a half is more effective than interventions started after the age of five (National Research Council, 2001). This is evident in the case of Carmen, who began receiving early intervention services at the age of two. By the time Carmen reached school age, many of his more severe characteristics of autism improved, which can be attributed to the early intervention services he received.

The Centers for Disease Control and Prevention (2015) and the American Academy of Pediatrics (2015) recommend that all children get screened for ASD at 18 and 24 months during well visits, and more often for those children who are at higher risk for ASD (e.g., family history). It is most likely that the child's pediatrician will administer the screening tools rather than an educational professional due to the early age recommendation.

The process of screening is not as labor intensive as other areas of assessment and requires less expertise compared to the evaluation and diagnostic processes. For instance, in many cases, the child's parent will complete the screening tool prior to the appointment and then be scored by the pediatrician.

The pediatrician only requires some knowledge of ASD to accurately score the screening tool. Most screening tools for ASD focus on social and communication impairments and are designed using criteria in the DSM-V. The DSM-V is published by the American Psychiatric Association (APA, 2013) and is used to diagnose mental and behavioral conditions.

However, prior to screening specifically for ASD, a child more than likely would have been screened using a developmental assessment tool. One common tool used in pediatrician offices is the *Ages and Stages Questionnaire*, Third Edition (ASQ-3; Squires et al., 2009) evaluation tool. This screening tool is organized around the domains of development, such as social, cognitive, language, adaptive, gross motor, and fine motor. Parents complete this questionnaire and note any areas of concern.

When Carmen's parents completed the 24-month ASQ-3, they marked numerous areas of concern that would justify further screening using a specific ASD tool. For instance, some areas of concern that they noted were: Carmen often does things repeatedly and gets upset when they try to stop him (hand flapping), he frequently has tantrums for long periods of time, rarely/never likes to be around other children, and is seldom interested in the things around him (ASQ-3; Squires et al., 2009). These results indicated that Carmen should most likely be screened using a tool specifically designed for ASD.

Online Screening Tools

One of the most widely known ASD screening tools is the Modified Checklist for Autism in Toddlers, Revised with Follow-Up (M-CHAT-R/F; Barton, Fein & Robins, 2009). It must be noted that M-CHAT-R/F should not be viewed as a diagnostic tool, but rather a tool that can identify potential children to be evaluated for a full diagnostic evaluation (Baird et al., 2000). The M-CHAT-R/F can be found online at: https://www.m-chat.org/, and is a two-stage parent-report screening tool used to assess risk for ASD. The M-CHAT-R/F consists of 20 questions with yes/no responses. This assessment is designed to identify toddlers and young children 16 to 30 months of age.

If the assessment results reveal a possible ASD diagnosis, it is recommended that the child receive, from a certified professional, a more thorough assessment for possible early signs of ASD or developmental delay. The M-CHAT is one of the assessment tools recommended by the American Academy of Pediatrics (AAP). The AAP recommends broad developmental screenings at intervals beginning at nine months of age (M-Chat.org, 2015).

Though screening tools are typically used with young children suspected of having ASD (16–30 months), tools are also available for older children and, in some cases, teenagers/adults. Many of these screening tools are found online and are easily located using any search engine. All of these downloadable assessments carry a warning for parents and guardians advising that, after the initial screening utilizing the online assessment, the results should be discussed with certified professionals. They also advise that the certified professional should conduct assessments to ascertain if the initial screening warrants further investigation.

One online assessment utilized by parents is the Asperger's Quiz. This 21-question assessment is designed to ascertain if the individual in question exhibits symptoms of Asperger's, formerly termed Asperger's syndrome. Asperger's is now part of the comprehensive ASD diagnosis. A unique aspect of this assessment is that it can be completed by teenagers or adults who may be unsure if they have any of the often-complex indicators of this disorder.

The Asperger's Quiz is divided into three categories: social symptoms, life skills, and physical (or behavioral) symptoms. Each subset details behaviors that could be attributed to an ASD diagnosis. The questions are answered in a "yes/no" format, and the quiz is scored and analyzed upon completion of the assessment (aspergersquiz.com, 2015).

Another online assessment is the Aspiranet Family Focused Quiz. This assessment is designed to assist parents and guardians in identifying behaviors commonly associated with ASD. The assessment can be administered to children as young as three years, up to a suggested ceiling age of 18. The 25 questions are answered as "mostly true" or "mostly false." Parents are requested to check the answer that most applies to their child. There is a disclaimer attached to the Aspiranet Family Focused Quiz that reminds parents that the instrument is designed to assist them only in identifying behaviors associated with ASD and is not to be used as a diagnostic tool. Parents are invited to contact the Aspiranet Organization to request a full ASD assessment (aspiranetffsn.org, 2015).

Several online assessments for ASD are now targeted toward teenagers and adults. An example of a "self-test" for ASD symptoms is the Short Autism Screening Test. This online assessment consists of 15 questions that are scored on a Likert scale (psychcentral.com, 2015). The respondents are asked to consider each question regarding whether or not the activity occurred at some time in their lives, and record their score. The scale is constructed to span childhood to adult behaviors. The assessment is automatically scored, and depending on the score, the respondent is rated. Ratings of "Autism Likely," "Autism Possible," and "No Autism" are determined from the corresponding scores. As with other online assessments, a disclaimer is present requesting that the respondent seek the assistance of a qualified professional, depending on the rating received.

The last online assessment discussed is the Autism Spectrum Quotient, or AQ assessment (archive.wired.com, 2015). As with the Short Autism Screening Test, this assessment is geared toward adults who may exhibit signs of ASD. This online assessment consists of 50 questions, scored on an agree/disagree Likert scale. The AQ is designed to measure the extent of autistic traits in adult respondents. The AQ is scored according to questions that were answered in either a positive or negative manner. Depending on the question number, a score of 1 point is calculated. Individuals whose score is 32 or higher on this 50-question assessment are considered to have mild autism. As with all of the other online assessments, individuals are cautioned to follow up with qualified professionals if they score at 32 or above in this assessment.

As previously stated, all one needs to do is Google "online assessments for autism," and several of the above assessment tools will appear, along with many other online assessment sites. This is not a discussion of the reliability or validity of these assessments. Nor is it a caution regarding the dangers of self-diagnosis. This is simply an informational description of what is available for both parents and caregivers to assist them in locating additional resources regarding their children's behaviors, before entering discussions with qualified professionals. Assessments geared to teenagers and adults should be utilized in the same fashion. They should be the starting point for discussions with qualified and certified professionals, who will then follow up with additional assessments that are both reliable and valid instruments for the diagnosis and classification of ASD.

DIAGNOSIS AND ELIGIBILITY

Once a child is suspected of having ASD, a full diagnostic evaluation occurs, consisting of multiple tests. Typically, these tests are the first formal tools administered to a child suspected of having ASD. The diagnostic assessment process can be enormously draining and emotional for parents. It is extremely important to walk parents through the steps of their child's evaluation and provide support throughout the process.

In the case of Carmen, his parents were extremely overwhelmed, emotional, and scared. Shortly after Carmen's pediatrician recommended a full evaluation completed by a developmental pediatrician, Carmen's parents contacted the local early intervention agency. The early intervention agency assigned Carmen a case manager. This case manager provided support to Carmen and his family and explained processes and results of tests. She provided resources and helped Carmen's family find a support group and network. After several meetings and conversations with his case manager, Carmen's parents began to feel less overwhelmed about the assessment process and Carmen's probable autism diagnosis.

Either the child's physician or local education agency (LEA) can initiate the evaluation process for ASD. In the case of Carmen, his physician initiated the evaluation process because this is where his parents brought up his first developmental concerns. For Maurice, on the other hand, the LEA initiated the evaluation (or in this case reevaluation, since Maurice already had a classification) because a teacher at the LEA was the first individual to notice a discrepancy between his behavior and his classification.

While the ultimate goal of a medical evaluation is to determine a medical or clinical diagnosis, the LEA provides a specific disability classification. The LEA classification determines if the student is eligible for special education services. Sometimes an LEA will use the term "educational determination of ASD" instead. The LEA provides an educational determination of ASD by interpreting the definition of ASD found in IDEA 2004, while the clinical diagnosis is performed by a medical professional—such as a physician, clinical psychologist, neurologist, psychiatrist, or developmental pediatrician—using criteria found in the DSM-V, along with a battery of other assessments.

It is important to note that educators in the LEA cannot give a clinical or medical diagnosis of ASD. In fact, there is no such thing as an educational diagnosis of autism! The LEA just determines the likelihood that a student has ASD. Both evaluation processes have benefits, so it is recommended that children receive both a clinical and educational evaluation when possible. As often happens, the ideal situation occurs when the medical field works collaboratively with the LEA's multidisciplinary team to diagnose a child with autism.

The following discussion will delve deeper into the medical and LEA evaluations and explore common tests used to diagnose autism. When the child's physician or other medical professional initiates the evaluation process for ASD, the following steps are typically taken:

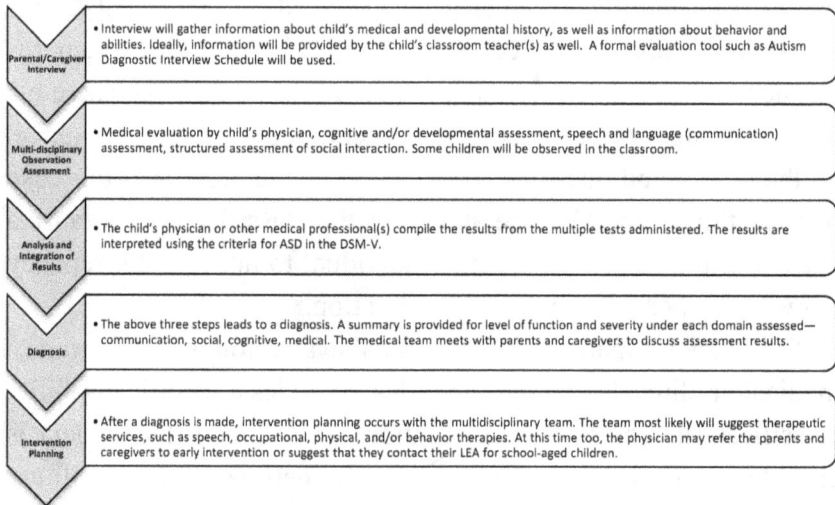

Parental/Caregiver Interview	• Interview will gather information about child's medical and developmental history, as well as information about behavior and abilities. Ideally, information will be provided by the child's classroom teacher(s) as well. A formal evaluation tool such as Autism Diagnostic Interview Schedule will be used.
Multi-disciplinary Observation Assessment	• Medical evaluation by child's physician, cognitive and/or developmental assessment, speech and language (communication) assessment, structured assessment of social interaction. Some children will be observed in the classroom.
Analysis and Integration of Results	• The child's physician or other medical professional(s) compile the results from the multiple tests administered. The results are interpreted using the criteria for ASD in the DSM-V.
Diagnosis	• The above three steps leads to a diagnosis. A summary is provided for level of function and severity under each domain assessed—communication, social, cognitive, medical. The medical team meets with parents and caregivers to discuss assessment results.
Intervention Planning	• After a diagnosis is made, intervention planning occurs with the multidisciplinary team. The team most likely will suggest therapeutic services, such as speech, occupational, physical, and/or behavior therapies. At this time too, the physician may refer the parents and caregivers to early intervention or suggest that they contact their LEA for school-aged children.

Figure 3.1.   The medical diagnosis process of ASD. *Source: Michelle Gonzalez, Carol Lee Maniscalco*

Best practice in the medical field indicates that the diagnosis process be multidisciplinary (Huerta & Lord, 2012). Multidisciplinary means that sources of information come from multiple areas and from multiple professionals, such as a physician, a speech language therapist, an occupational therapist, physical therapist, and a developmental psychologist. Though best practice indicates that multiple professionals take part in the evaluation process, there are instances where only one medical professional conducts the evaluation.

Parents and caregivers should be prepared for the time commitment of the medical evaluation process. The entire evaluation process can take several hours and more than one appointment. In addition, it can take weeks, and in some instances a few months, to get an appointment to be evaluated for autism. Luckily, parents and caregivers do not need to wait for an official diagnosis to get help. While waiting for a diagnosis, the child can still be evaluated by an early intervention agency or LEA, and get appropriate support and services, such as speech/language therapy, occupational therapy, and physical therapy.

In Carmen's case, he was diagnosed with ASD at an early age. Some individuals question the accuracy of diagnosing a child with autism at such a young age, but research has shown that a diagnosis of autism at age two can be reliable, valid, and stable (CDC, 2015). After screening at a "high risk" level for autism, Carmen's pediatrician referred his parents to a developmental pediatrician in a nearby city. Unfortunately, the wait for an initial appointment was two months!

This concerned Carmen's parents. They knew that he needed help. His pediatrician suggested that they call the local early intervention agency. The agency could perform a developmental evaluation of Carmen and identify areas of need. This would allow him to begin early intervention services while waiting for an autism diagnosis.

Carmen was assessed using Hawaii Early Learning Profile for ages 0–3 (HELP: 0–3; Parks, 2006), a common criterion-referenced assessment used in early intervention. Results of the test indicated that he had significant delays in the language, social-emotional, and gross motor domains. The early intervention team developed an intervention plan called an Individual Family Service Plan (IFSP) for Carmen, and he began receiving services in his home even before his appointment with the developmental pediatrician.

After a few months of receiving early intervention services, Carmen finally received a formal diagnosis of autism. In addition to the existing early intervention services he was receiving, he began occupational therapy to address some of his sensory issues, and applied behavior analysis (ABA) to help decrease his tantrum behavior.

Carmen is an example of one child who was diagnosed with autism prior to entering the school system. Many children today are still found by their LEA to have autism (Braiden, Bothwell & Duffy, 2010). Most of these students identified by the LEA usually have higher-functioning autism. As stated previously, the medical field makes a clinical diagnosis of autism, while the educational system provides an educational determination, or a classification, of autism.

It is extremely important that the educational professionals classifying students with ASD receive training in the DSM-V, are proficient with administering and interpreting ASD diagnostic tools, and have the professional judgment to distinguish ASD from other disabilities with similar characteristics. Noland and Gabriels (2004) recommend that educational professionals should be cautious, and only operate within their scope of training and experience when classifying students with ASD. They should also keep close ties with medical professionals who can help eliminate any biological or neurological cause of the disability. Again, this is one reason why both a clinical and educational evaluation is recommended to ensure that children are not classified incorrectly with autism.

Parents and family members who accept a misdiagnosis or an incorrect classification of ASD tend to treat the child differently because they assume that the child exhibits ASD tendencies. Unfortunately, when this occurs, the child is sometimes denied many of the social interactions or developmental opportunities needed by young children on the spectrum. These children are then unable to develop the appropriate skills required to advance academically and socially.

Remember Maurice, the boy who was classified incorrectly as having autism? While his academic progress improved tremendously upon getting a proper individual educational plan, his assimilation into the school's general population was more difficult. This was due to having remained in self-contained class environments throughout the lower grades, where his only social contact was with other isolated students. Maurice never had the opportunity or encouragement to develop social skills and build friendships. He simply reflected the social disconnectedness modeled by his fellow classmates, leaving him ill prepared to interact with his general population peers. Correct diagnosis and classification is critical, and it is hoped that all parents and guardians will bring their concerns to certified professionals who can conduct further assessments to ascertain if the parents' concerns are valid.

Like the medical evaluation, specific steps are followed when completing an educational evaluation for ASD, as well as for other SDs. First, once a child has been identified as having difficulty in the classroom and pre-referral interventions have been unsuccessful, or the child has been brought to the authorities' attention through a district child-find program, the task of evaluating the child begins. According to federal statutes (IDEA, 2007), once parental consent is obtained, a multifaceted assessment process is started. Formal, standardized assessments, along with direct observation and informal methods, are conducted. The formal assessments include both autism-specific tests and tests that measure general ability and behavior (achievement, speech/language, cognitive behavior, etc.). These various assessment methods are compiled, and eligibility for special education and related services under the classification category of autism is determined.

Once a classification of autism is determined, the multidisciplinary team, consisting of CST/MDT members, instructional staff, parents, and administrators, creates an IEP for the student. The student's educational placement, along with related services that the student needs in order to advance academically, is decided. If a student is not found eligible for special education under the classification of autism or any other disability, he/she is still eligible to receive assistance (accommodations and modifications) in the classroom under Section 504 of the Rehabilitation Act.

Figure 3.2 provides a modified visual representation of the educational evaluation process of ASD.

Additionally, the IEP delineates the methods of continued progress monitoring that will be conducted by the classroom instructors. In accordance with IDEA, all students participate in statewide and district-wide assessments. However, the methods of accommodations and modifications that the student requires are also delineated in the IEP document (Heward, 2013).

This is a modified version of the special needs assessment process but is presented so that an understanding of the terms related to classroom assessment is aligned with the special needs assessment and classification process.

The previous figure illustrates the educational process of classifying a student with ASD. Now many parents wonder what to do when they receive a medical diagnosis of ASD and have not received an evaluation conducted by the LEA. It is important to note that a parent can bring a medical diagnosis of ASD to the local LEA and request an evaluation. The parent can request an evaluation by calling or writing either the director of special education or the principal of their child's school.

Even though the child has a medical diagnosis of ASD, an LEA will still evaluate the child to see if the disability impacts learning/ education. There are some rare cases where a physician diagnoses a child with ASD, but the school system fails to classify the student

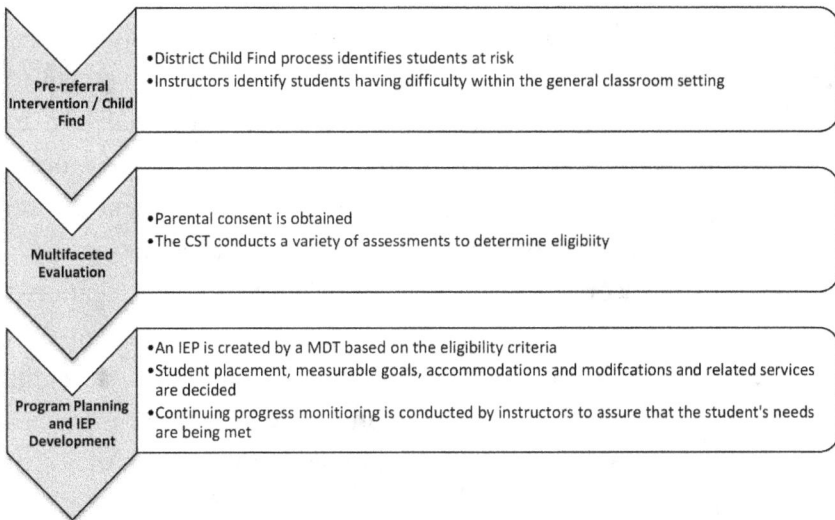

Figure 3.2. Modified educational planning process. *Source: Michelle Gonzalez, Carol Lee Maniscalco*

with ASD. The school more than likely found that the child's educational performance was not impacted by his disability. This does not mean that the child does not have ASD. It only means that it does not impact educational performance and the student does not require an individual education plan. However, in more cases than not, a child will receive both a medical diagnosis and educational determination of ASD.

In the case of Carmen, when he was transitioning to preschool at age three, his parents contacted the local school district's special education director and requested an evaluation, which was granted. Carmen was reevaluated again by the school district when he was transitioning to kindergarten. In both instances, he still qualified for special education services under the classification of autism. At age three, Carmen was placed in a preschool class specifically designated for children with autism in his local school district. Here he received intense interventions to help him continue to learn new skills and to develop.

When Carmen transitioned to kindergarten, many of his more severe autistic behaviors (self-injurious behavior and tantrum behavior) were almost extinct, and he showed great improvement in his language development. These improvements allowed him to successfully participate in an inclusion kindergarten classroom. Carmen's parents were thrilled and knew the early intervention and preschool services helped him reach this level of success!

Again, it is recommended that both a clinical and educational evaluation occur. The educational evaluation guides student programming, helps develop an IEP, and identifies a child's strengths and weaknesses. Simply, it helps plan for school-based interventions. Nevertheless, there are more similarities than differences in the medical and educational diagnosis of autism. For further information regarding the comparison of the medical and LEA evaluation of ASD, please refer to table 3.1. What is most important is that both evaluations keep the child's best interests in mind and help the child reach his/her greatest potential.

TOOLS FOR DIAGNOSING ASD

The following section will discuss common tools used to diagnose an individual with autism. Again, best practice indicates that the diagnostic process in both the medical and educational fields take into account multiple sources utilizing many different forms of measurement tools (Huerta & Lord, 2012; Gotham, Bishop & Lord, 2011). Thus, information is collected about the child's behavior and development in the form of observations, interviews, and scales.

The multidisciplinary evaluation will most likely consist of cognitive development, adaptive behavior, language or speech, and autism-specific assessments. Both the medical and educational field can use these autism-specific tools, but specific training is necessary to accurately administer and interpret the results. Com-

Table 3.1.   A comparison of medical diagnosis and educational evaluation of ASD.

Medical Evaluation	Educational Evaluation
Diagnosis of autism using DSM-V criteria	Educational determination of autism using IDEA
Determines adaptive functioning	Determines educational functioning
Multidisciplinary team, but in some cases a single medical professional makes diagnosis.	Multidisciplinary or child study team determines eligibility.
Uses multiple tests including an autism specific measure. Uses observations, interviews, testing.	Uses multiple tests including an autism-specific measure. Uses observations, interviews, testing.
A medical professional conducts diagnosis, such as a developmental pediatrician, board certified psychologist, or psychiatrist.	Educational professional conducts evaluations, such as a school psychologist.
Recommends specific therapeutic interventions to address specific nature of the child's problem, such as physical, occupational, speech, and behavior therapies.	Develops an individual education plan consisting of specially designed instruction, strategies, services, and accommodations to allow child to have success in the educational setting.

mon diagnostic tools utilized in both the medical and educational field include:

- Childhood Autism Rating Scale, Second Edition (CARS-2)
- Autism Diagnostic Interview Schedule-Revised (ADI-R)
- Autism Diagnostic Observation Schedule, Second Edition (ADOS-2)

The CARS-2 (Schopler, Van Bourgondien, Wellman & Love, 2010) helps identify children with autism beginning at age two, and determines symptom severity through direct observations. It is one of the most widely used tools to diagnose autism (Schopler et al., 2010). The test consists of a parent questionnaire and a rating scale to be completed by the child's physician or other qualified professional. There are two rating scales in the CARS-2, each consisting of 15 items.

The Standard Version Rating scale is for children younger than six years old, or who demonstrate difficulties with communication, or who have below-average estimated IQ scores. The high-functioning version rating scale is for children older than six, with estimated IQ scores of greater than 80.

Testing items consist of functional areas such as relating to people, adaptation to change, verbal and nonverbal communication, emotional response, body use, and use of objects. Each of the 15 items is rated on a scale from 1 (within normal limits for the age) to 4 (severely abnormal use of the behavior for age). The parental questionnaire is not scored, but it does help the physician complete either of the rating scales. After the interview, it only takes approximately 5–10 minutes to score.

A second common diagnostic tool is the Autism Diagnostic Interview Schedule-Revised (ADI-R; Lord, Rutter & Le Couteur, 1994), which consists of a semi-structured interview for parents or caregivers. This test can be used for a formal diagnosis, treatment planning, and educational planning for children and adults with a mental age above two. Administration requires an experienced and competent interviewer, as well as an individual who has experience with autism (Gotham et al., 2011). Administration and coding of the instrument takes from 90–150 minutes. Thus, it is suggested that parents may want to use a sitter or caregiver to watch their child rather than bring their child to the interview appointment.

The interview consists of 93 items in the following content areas:

- The subject's background, including family, education, previous diagnoses, and medications
- Overview of the subject's behavior
- Early development and developmental milestones
- Language acquisition and loss of language or other skills
- Current functioning in regard to language and communication
- Social development and play

- Interests and behaviors
- Clinically relevant behaviors, such as aggression, self-injury, and possible epileptic features.

After the interview, the physician, most likely a psychologist or psychiatrist, codes the interview and reports the results under the categorical domains of language/communication, social reciprocity, and repetitive behavior/interests.

The third diagnostic tool is the Autism Diagnostic Observation Schedule, Second Edition (ADOS-2; Lord, Rutter et al., 2010), which is often used jointly with the ADI-R. The ADOS-2 is considered the benchmark of the diagnostic processes for ASD (Lord & Corsello, 2005). It allows individuals to be assessed and diagnosed with ASD across ages, developmental levels, and language skills. Unlike the CARS-2 and ADI-R, the ADOS-2 allows for direct assessment of toddlers, children, and adults suspected of having autism.

The ADOS-2 has five levels or modules of administration, and a specific module for toddlers. Selecting the appropriate module to use is dependent upon the expressive language skill and chronological age of the individual getting evaluated. The individual is only assessed in one module.

The modules are as follows:

- Toddler Module: Children between 12 and 30 months of age who do not consistently use phrase speech
- Module 1: Children 31 months and older who do not consistently use phrase speech
- Module 2: Children of any age who use phrase speech but are not verbally fluent
- Module 3: Verbally fluent children and young adolescents
- Module 4: Verbally fluent older adolescents and adults

Each module consists of a series of activities to complete with the examinee. A few activity examples from Module 3 are: make-believe play, joint interactive play, cartoons, emotions, and friends. A stimulus kit with needed materials is provided to help implement the activities. This kit includes items such as toys, dolls, books, and manipulatives. Immediately after each activity, the results are coded and scored using an algorithm. The algorithm scores are compared with cutoff scores resulting in the classification of autism, autism spectrum, or non-spectrum. The toddler module only reports ranges of concern instead of a distinct classification, as in Modules 1–4. The ADOS-2 is the most complex of diagnostic tools discussed in this chapter, thus it is recommended that an expert and experienced team administer and discuss the results (Overton, 2012).

Again, it must be noted that the above diagnostic tools are only one piece of the multidisciplinary assessment process. The child will still be assessed for cognitive ability, behavior, medical history, speech/language, and adaptive behavior. Results of these assessments will lead to the identification of the child's strengths and weaknesses, which will help with intervention and program planning.

For instance, after Carmen's results of the CARS-2 were interpreted, it was determined that he had difficulty with pretend play and using objects for play. Based on this information, Carmen's intervention team ensured that there were plenty of opportunities in his therapeutic play sessions involving the modeling and practice of this skill.

Finally, the diagnostic process for ASD, or any other disability, can be overwhelming. It is suggested that parents and caregivers take notes during the process, or ask someone to take notes. It may also be beneficial to have a social worker present, to help alleviate concerns or explain results in a more parent-friendly way. A babysitter or caregiver for the child may be a good idea, allowing parents to focus on the results and ask questions without having to worry about watching their child.

CLASSROOM ASSESSMENTS

Once a child receives an ASD classification and begins receiving services, the focus of assessment shifts. Assessment becomes more closely tied to instruction and interventions. For instance, in the classroom assessment results are used for instructional planning, progress status, and progress monitoring. These assessments often occur in the classroom and are completed by the student's teachers.

Instruction in the classroom is continually assessed in both a formative and summative manner. The most popular methods of instruction, applied behavior analysis and discrete trial (DT) instruction, have assessment methods that are conducted along with the instruction. These two methods are discussed in the chapters dealing with classroom instruction.

Even though the above techniques are commonly used with the ASD population, other techniques are also used effectively during instruction. These techniques include both standardized, and criterion-referenced instruments. Instructors have found that continual assessment of ASD students is necessary, to assure the continuum of learning and the retention of necessary material. As more and more data is collected in the classroom, the use of additional assessments, with easy to use, effective instruments for measuring and recording the achievement of ASD students, has proved helpful to instructors.

Some of the assessments utilized by instructors in both the elementary and secondary level include: district benchmarks, the Assessment of Basic Language and Learning Skills (ABLLS-Revised), the Verbal Behavior Milestones Assessment and Placement Program (VB-MAPP), the Wide Range Achievement Test (WRAT-4 Green & Blue form), the Brigance Comprehensive Inventory of Basic Skills II (CIBS II), the School Social Skills Rating Scale (S3 Rating Scale), and Social Skills Improvement System (SSIS) Rating Scales.

District benchmarks are simply measurement instruments (usually paper and pencil assessments) that are to be administered four times per year to track the progress of students. They are mandated by the school district. District committees or individual school teams typically create benchmark assessments. They are used to assess the progress of individual students as they move through the grade-level curriculum.

Teachers of ASD students use the benchmark assessments to track students' progress as they move through their aligned grade-level curriculum. Many times, districts require benchmarks from all students, regardless of disabilities. It is the responsibility of the teacher to correctly align the benchmark assessment to the individual student's functional grade level, as well as provide the accommodations and modifications for testing, as required by the IEP. The results of the benchmark assessments are utilized to track students' retention of material as they progress through their aligned grade level.

For instance, in the case of Maurice, his teacher utilized district benchmark assessments for reading, writing, and math. Maurice's functional grade level for all three subject areas was far below what was expected for a typical 12-year-old. Therefore, he received benchmark tests that were aligned with his level. He also needed accommodations, such as having the test directions and questions read to him and having extended time to complete the tests. This alignment to his functional level, and the additional accommodations, ensured that these assessments would give an accurate picture of his growth and abilities.

Classroom teachers also use the Assessment of Basic Language and Learning Skills-Revised (ABLLS-R) (Partington, 2015) to continually assess students' progress during the school term. When needed, the ABLLS-R can be also used as a stand-alone curriculum guide. This assessment contains a guide for tracking communication and critical learning skills, identifying 25 skill areas, broken up into 544 individual skills that are needed by students in order to be successful in a classroom setting. Pre-readiness skills, such as language, social interactions, self-help, motor, and academic skills, are identified and assessed. The ABLLS-R is usually utilized in preschool, kindergarten, and early primary settings as it is geared to pre-kindergarten readiness skills (Partington, 2015).

The ABLLS-R has a two-part system consisting of the Protocol and the Guide. The protocol document contains sets of grids that create an individual tracking system to document the students' progress as they advance through the school year. The guide document gives detailed instructions for the scoring of the assessment items, and can also be utilized by teachers and CST/MDT and IEP teams to plan for future IEP instructional goals and objectives, based on students' results (Partington, 2015).

Classroom teachers also utilize the Verbal Behavior Milestones Assessment and Placement Program (VB-MAPP) developed by Mark L. Sundberg, Ph.D. The VB-MAPP is a criterion-referenced instrument that, like the ABLLS-R, can be utilized as a skill-tracking system as well as a stand-alone curriculum. The VB-MAPP Milestones Assessment is available in three developmental levels: 0–18 months, 18–30 months, and 30–48 months (Sundberg, 2015).

Most instructors focus on the 30–48 month milestone assessment that pinpoints social and academic pre-readiness skills that are key for student success in the classroom environment. Personnel are able to administer the assessment through either observation or direct testing. The results of the VB-MAPP can be used to establish a baseline, track acquisition of individual skills, and provide a guide for implementing future goals and objectives for individual students.

Classroom instructors may also rely on the Wide Range Achievement Test (WRAT-4) to assess progress in the core content academic areas of reading, spelling, arithmetic, and science. The WRAT-4 is aligned to skills and grade-based norms in grades K–12. This is instrumental in facilitating classroom teachers' use of the instrument (Wilkinson & Robertson, 2006).

The WRAT-4 is a standardized assessment that provides a scripted test for examiners to follow. Classroom teachers can derive a raw score and compare it to the standard score, utilizing preset norms based on age and grade levels. As with previous assessments mentioned here, instructors utilize scores from the WRAT-4 to track progress, remediate when needed, and plan for future IEP goals and objectives. The data provided by the WRAT is also useful in aligning to grade- and age-level norms, allowing educators to define the academic ability levels of individual students.

The Brigance Assessment Batteries is another frequent resource for classroom teachers, support personnel, and CSTs/MDTs in assessing students' abilities, planning instructional goals, and providing data for in-class instruction. The Brigance Assessment System consists of several different assessments, ranging from Early Developmental Skills to Transition Skills. However the Brigance CIBS II (Comprehensive Inventory of Basic Skills II) is the most commonly used instrument by classroom personnel, both for tracking student achievement and planning for individual instructional objectives.

The Brigance CIBS II includes an English Language Arts (ELA)/Reading and Mathematics Inventory. The ELA inventory measures students' abilities in a variety of subtests including: reading readiness, speech, vocabulary listening skills, and comprehension abilities. Word recognition, oral reading skills, spelling, writing, and response to writing prompts are also included. The Mathematics portion contains five subtests, including number operations, algebra, geometry, measurement, and data analysis (Curriculum Associates, 2015).

In all, there are over 400 criterion-referenced assessment tasks in the CIBS II that simplify the process used by instructional personnel to identify present levels of learning, along with providing specific educational data to align with ongoing instruction. Because they are criterion-referenced, the assessments may be used both by instructors and support personnel. The design of the instrument allows for several administrations during the school year, making it possible for instructional staff to track the students' progress throughout the term. Many districts utilize the Brigance CIBS II as a benchmark instrument to chart progress at specific times during the school year.

Finally, two in-class assessment tools helpful to classroom teachers are the School Social Skills Rating Scale (S3 Rating Scale) and the Social Skills Improvement System (SSIS) Rating Scales. These assessments, which are typically used together, identify student deficits in school-related social behaviors. The S3 allows teachers to identify a student's current abilities in the areas of school-related social skills. The S3 is an observable scored instrument that can be administered by either the teacher or classroom aide, as can the SSIS assessment (Pearson Clinical, 2015).

The SSIS measures not only specific social skills such as communication, cooperation, responsibility, and self-control, but also addresses two other areas: academic competences and competing problem behaviors. Academic competences such as reading, arithmetic, and self-motivation are assessed, and competing problem behaviors such as externalized bullying, hyperactivity, and internalized autism spectrum behaviors are measured (Pearson Clinical, 2015).

The SSIS allows instructional personnel to assess individuals and small groups in order to identify personal behaviors that impede personal and academic progress. In addition, the SSIS has parent and student forms to provide a comprehensive assessment of the student across three environments: home, school, and community (Pearson Clinical, 2015).

Similar to the discussion regarding online ASD assessments, classroom teachers utilize many in-class assessment instruments to measure student progress and plan continued instruction. Sometimes the use of a specific assessment is dictated by the school district, or the components of an IEP are mandated by the CST/MDT. Other times the assessment is dictated simply by the amount of money budgeted for classroom supplies.

Some teachers develop their own checklist assessments, relying on observation and curriculum benchmarks. For instance, Carmen's preschool teacher developed a set of tables to record the frequency and duration of his self-injurious behavior. After recording the behavior, she transferred the data to a line graph. Over time, she was able to see that the frequency and duration of his behavior was decreasing by analyzing the downward slope of the plotted data points, which illustrated the success of Carmen's interventions. Whatever method is utilized to assess students with ASD, instructors must strive to find a user-friendly and effective assessment system that will work in their classroom, providing the best possible feedback to facilitate the instructional advancement of their students.

Occasionally, the assessments dictated for ASD/SD students fail to take into account the realities of teaching "on the front lines." One middle school teacher, when tasked with applying a standardized end-of-grade test to a very low-functioning student with autism, followed her instructions to the letter. The student was given the test paper, and the timer was started.

The student was completely nonverbal and totally incapable of understanding the test instructions. The teacher had begged for accommodations, but they were denied. As the timer ticked down to the end of the test, the bored student had jammed the test paper into his mouth and chewed on it until the teacher finally pried it from his mouth. The test was sealed in plastic wrap and was sent to the district office, along with other tests from that day!

This example is an unfortunate story and illustrates an occasion where the assessment process did not benefit the student. However, there are more times than not when the assessment process results in positive outcomes, as in the cases of Maurice and Carmen. In the example above, the student did not receive accommodations. But in many cases, students with ASD will receive appropriate accommodations for both formal and informal tests. These accommodations may be in the form of extended time, a distraction-free environment, breaks, directions and test questions read aloud, and modified or alternative tests.

SUMMARY

The assessment process is a key component in the education of a student with ASD. It begins with an initial screening test that can be completed by a parent or caregiver and interpreted by a medical or education professional. The process then shifts to the medical diagnosis and/or determination of eligibility of ASD. The child's physician makes a diagnosis of autism, while educational professionals determine if the child qualifies for special education under the classification of autism. It is important to have a strong support person or group, and possible advocate, through the assessment process. It can be overwhelming and scary for a parent to have their child go through multiple tests and find out he/she has been assessed with autism. A strong support group or individual will help to alleviate some of this stress.

Once an official diagnosis and/or educational determination of autism is made, the child begins to receive interventions and/or special education services. Once special education services begin, classroom assessment takes center stage in the assessment process.

In the classroom, assessment is closely tied to instruction. Classroom assessment can be both informal and formal. It is used to plan instruction and monitor progress toward goals. When careful consideration is made in the assessment process, positive outcomes are likely, as seen in the cases of Carmen and Maurice.

EXERCISES AND APPLICATIONS

ASD Screening Tools

Many ASD screening tools are found online, making them very accessible to parents, caregivers, and educators. It is important to become familiar with these screening tools in order to gain a better understanding of their nature and to make informed decisions. In this activity, download, review, and complete a few of the screening tools discussed in the chapter in order to gain a full perspective of the tool. You may use someone you know who has ASD or who is suspected of having ASD when completing the test. After completing a few of the screening tools, reflect on the following questions:

- How do the items in the screening tools you reviewed compare to the characteristics of ASD?
- How were the screening tools you reviewed similar and different? Did the tools yield useful information?
- What recommendations do you have for educators, parents, and caregivers in the use of these screening tools?

ASD Screening Resources

M-CHAT: https://m-chat.org
Aspergers Quiz: http://aspergersquiz.com
Autism Quiz: http://www.aspiranetffsn.org/autism-quiz/
Autism Spectrum Quotient: http://archive.wired.com/wired/archive/9.12/aqtest.html

Short Autism Screening Test: http://psychcentral.com/quizzes/
autism-quiz.htm

Case Study: What would you do?

Read and review the following case study about Jessica. Answer
the questions found at the end of the case study.

Jessica is a three-year-old girl. Jessica's parents report that she
met the required developmental milestones from birth to 15
months. She was able to say single words (*dada, mama, ball*, etc.)
at 12 months and speak in simple two-word phrases by 15 months.
At approximately 18 months, Jessica's parents noticed a change in
her language and behavior. Jessica became very quiet and stopped
using the language she had acquired. She also began losing interest
in playing with her older sister and appeared to be in her own little
world. Eventually, she stopped responding to her name. At that
time, Jessica's parents were referred to early intervention services,
and she began receiving speech and language therapy at age two.

Now, at the age of three, Jessica still does not have language,
cannot use gestures to communicate her needs, and does not demonstrate pretend play. Jessica also demonstrates other behaviors,
such as having difficulty sleeping, and screaming when she hears
the vacuum or lawn mower. Jessica likes to repeatedly line up her
stuffed animals and gets agitated when one appears out of place.
Jessica's speech therapist is concerned, and suggests that she get
evaluated for ASD. Jessica's parents are overwhelmed and do not
know how to proceed.

- Is Jessica's behavior and development typical? Why or why not?
  What characteristics of ASD is Jessica exhibiting?
- Do you feel that it is warranted for Jessica to be screened and
  evaluated for ASD? Why or why not?

- What comprehensive assessment plan would you recommend for Jessica? In your plan, consider screening, diagnostic evaluations, educational evaluations, and classroom assessment.
- What recommendations do you have for Jessica and her parents?

REFERENCES

ABBLS-R. (April 11, 2015). Retrieved from http://www.partingtonbehavioranalysts.com/page/ablls-r-25.html.
American Psychiatric Association. (2013). *Diagnostic and statistical manual of mental disorders*: DSM-5. Washington, DC: American Psychiatric Association Aspire. (April 14, 2015). Retrieved from http:/www.aspiranetffsn.org/autism-quiz/austim-quiz-3-to-18-years/. (April 14, 2015). Retrieved from http://aspergersquiz.com/Autism Spectrum Quotient. (May 27, 2015). Retrieved from http://archive.wired.com/wired/archive/9.12/aqtest.htm.
Baird, G., Charman, T., Baron-Cohen, S., Cox, A., Swettenham, J., Wheelwright, S., & Drew, A. (2000). A screening instrument for autism at 18 months of age: A 6-year follow-up study. *J. Am. Acad. Child Adolesc. Psychiatry*, *39*(6), 694–702.
Barton, Fein, & Robins. (2009). *Modified Checklist for Autism in Toddlers, Revised with Follow-Up*. Retrieved from https://www.m-chat.org.
Boyd, B. A., & Shaw, E. (2010). Autism in the classroom: A group of students changing in population and presentation. *Preventing School Failure*, *54*(4), 211–19.
Braiden, H. J., Bothwell, J., & Duffy, J. (2010). Parents' experience of the diagnostic process for autistic spectrum disorders. *Child Care in Practice*, *16*(4), 377–89.
Brigance Comprehensive Inventory of Basic Skills II. (April 11, 2015). Retrieved from http://www.curriculumassociates.com/products/detail.aspx?title=brigcibsii.
Centers for Disease Control and Prevention. (2015). Autism: Screening and Diagnosis. Retrieved from http://www.cdc.gov/ncbddd/autism/screening.html.
Charles, C., & Senter, G. (2012). *Elementary classroom management*, 6th ed. Boston: Pearson.
Criterion Referenced Assessment: What is Criterion Referenced Assessment. (May 25, 2015). Retrieved from http://www.unm.edu/~devalenz/handouts/criterion.html.
Definition of reliability and validity. (May 27, 2015). Retrieved from http://rlhoover.people.ysu.edu/OAT-OGT/reliability_validity.html.
Durocher, J. Assessment for the Purpose of Instructional Planning. (May 1, 2015). Retrieved from http://www.ocali.org/up_doc/Assessment_for_the_Purpose_of_Instructional_Planning_for_ASD.pdf.

Gotham, K., Bishop, S. L., & Lord, C. (2011). Diagnosis of autism spectrum disorders. In D. G. Amaral, G. Dawson, & D. H. Geschwind (Eds.), *Autism spectrum disorders* (pp. 30–43). New York: Oxford University Press.

Heward, W. (2013). *Exceptional children: An introduction to special education,* 10th ed. Boston: Pearson.

Huerta, M., & Lord, C. (2012). Diagnostic evaluation of autism spectrum disorders. *Pediatric Clinical North America, 59*(1), 103–11.

IEP Referral. Understanding Special Education. (April 11, 2015). Retrieved from http://www.understandingspecialeducation.com/IEP-referral.html.

Jennings, J. H., Caldwell, J. S., & Lerner, J. W. (2006). *Reading Problems: Assessment and Teaching Strategies (5th ed.)*. Boston: Allyn & Bacon.

Linn, R. L., & Gronlund, N. E. (2000). *Measurement and assessment in teaching,* 8th ed. Upper Saddle River, NJ: Prentice Hall.

Lord, C., Rutter, M., & Le Couteur, A. (1994). Autism Diagnostic Interview-Revised: A revised version of a diagnostic interview for caregivers of individuals with possible pervasive developmental disorders. *Journal of Autism and Developmental Disorders, 24*: 659–85.

Lord, C., & Corsello, C. (2005). Diagnostic instruments in autistic spectrum disorders. In F. Volkmar, R. Paul, A. Klin, & D. Cohen (Eds.), *Handbook of autism and pervasive developmental disorders* (pp. 730–71). Somerset, NJ: Wiley.

Lord, C., Rutter, M., et al. (2010). *Autism Diagnostic Observation Schedule,* 2nd ed. Torrance, CA: WPS Publishing.

M-CHAT Autism Assessment. (May 1, 2015). Retrieved from https://www.m-chat.org/.

National Research Council. (2001). Educating Children with Autism. Retrieved from http://www.nap.edu/catalog/10017.html.

Noland, R. M., & Gabriels, R. L. (2004). Screening and identifying children with autism spectrum disorders in the public school system: The development of a model process. *Journal of Autism & Developmental Disorders, 34*(3), 265–77.

Overton, T. (2012). *Assessing learners with special needs: An applied approach.* New York: Pearson.

Parks, S. W. (2006). *Hawaii Early Learning Profile: 0–3.* Menlow Park, CA: Vort Corporation.

School Social Skills Rating Scales (S3). (May 1, 2015). Retrieved from http://www.amazon.com/School-Social-Skills-Rating-Paperback/dp/B000FNU2QE.

Schopler, E., Van Bourgondien, M. E., Wellman, G. J., & Love, S. R. (2010). *The Childhood Autism Rating Scale-Second edition* (CARS2). Los Angeles: Western Psychological Services.

Short Aspergers Screening Test. (May 1, 2015). Retrieved from http://psychcentral.com/quizzes/autism-quiz.

Short Autism Screening Test. (May 1, 2015). Retrieved from http://psychcentral.com/quizzes/autism-quiz.

90 *Gonzalez and Maniscalco*

Social Skills Improvement System Rating Scales (SSIS). (May 1, 2015). Retrieved from http://www.pearsonclinical.com/education/products/100000322/social-skills-improvement-system-ssis-rating-scales.html#tab-details.

Spinelli, C. (2012). *Classroom assessment for students in special education and general education*, 3rd ed. Boston: Pearson.

Squires, J., Bricker, D., Twombly, E., Nickel, R., Clifford, J., Murphy, K., Hoselton, R., Potter, L., Mounts, L., & Farrell, J. (2009). *Ages & stages questionnaires*, 3rd ed. (ASQ-3). Baltimore: Paul H. Brookes.

Verbal Behavior Milestones Assessment and Placement Program (VB-MAPP). (May 1, 2015). Retrieved from http://www.marksundberg.com/vb-mapp.htm.

Wide Range Achievement Test 4, Green Form (WRAT-4). (May 1, 2015). Retrieved from http://www.academictherapy.com/detailATP.tpl?eqskudatarq=DDD-946&.

Wilkinson, G. S. & Robertson, G. J. (2006). *Wide Range Achievement Test 4*. Lutz, FL: Psychological Assessment Resources.

Chapter Four

Challenging Behaviors

Jeanne D'Haem

Sometimes Billy would grab his teacher's hair and not let go. He was strong enough to yank a handful out by the roots. Like many students on the autism spectrum and those with developmental disabilities, he exhibited very challenging behaviors.

This chapter discusses the behavioral characteristics of students like Billy with ASD and other developmental disorders. It includes behavior assessments and evidence-based interventions. It also covers the importance of antecedent management strategies involving differential reinforcement, video instruction, and social stories. Interventions for physical agitation, aversive stimuli, and medical interventions will be discussed. We will meet some individuals like Billy and learn how more effective interventions were found.

Autism is a spectrum disorder. That means it encompasses a wide variety of abilities and challenges (Iovannone, Dunlap, Huber & Kincaid, 2003). Students with autism spectrum disorder (ASD) can be low functioning, nonverbal, preoccupied with a few objects, and, like Billy, exhibit aggressive behaviors. Others are able to function independently, have good intellectual abilities, and initiate social interactions. Students with other developmental disabilities have a range of abilities and challenges as well.

The Individuals with Disabilities Education Act of 1990 identifies autistic characteristics as engagement in repetitive activities, stereotyped movements, resistance to change or routine, and unusual responses to sensory experiences. Many of the characteristics associated with ASD fall into three core deficit areas: 1) communication, 2) socialization, and 3) repetitive interests and behaviors. Scheuermann and Webber (2002) describe the behaviors of those with ASD in two broad groups: behavioral deficits, or the inability to relate to others, lack of functional language, sensory processing deficits, and cognitive deficits; and behavioral excesses, such as self-stimulation, resistance to change, bizarre or challenging behaviors, and self-injurious behaviors. This chapter will focus on behavioral excesses.

Observations

If you work with students with ASD or DD (developmental disabilities), what challenging behaviors have you observed on the triad of deficits?

1. Communication: echolalia, pronoun reversal, delayed verbalizations, or no language.

   - _____
   - _____
   - _____

2. Socialization: unaware of the presence of others, no orientation to voices, sharing only facts about preferred topic.

   - _____
   - _____
   - _____

3. Behavior: insistence on sameness including food and clothing, repetitive movements, unusual reactions to sensory stimuli such as loud noises, under responsive to pain, tactile defensiveness, hitting, biting, or screaming.

- _____
- _____
- _____

Problem behaviors may include noncompliance, perseverative actions, and aggressive behaviors such as spitting, biting, or hitting. Unfortunately, some children display self-injurious actions such a biting their hand, hair pulling, or head banging. People with ASD become easily overaroused in situations that are stressful to them, and once overstimulated, they remain so for extended periods.

For example, Michael's parents got into some traffic on their way to take their son with ASD to a baseball game. They sprinted from the parking lot into the ballpark but still missed the opening pitch. Michael was obsessed with baseball. It is the only thing he wanted to talk about. When he realized the game had already started he began to scream and cry. He would not be comforted or distracted. His behavior disrupted everyone sitting around the family in the stadium. Even when he was told that if he did not stop screaming they would have to leave, he did not stop. The family had to go home because he did not calm down.

Due to such difficult behaviors, individuals with ASD and developmental delays face significant impairment in the areas of independent living, employment, and social and romantic relationships. They also suffer from high rates of comorbid psychiatric diagnoses and other mental health problems. When we compare them to typically developing peers, adults with Asperger's disorder have indicated that they have a lower quality of life.

Billy's parents once took him to a movie, but he grabbed the hair of a woman who sat in the row in front of him and would not let go. Obviously, they could not take him to the movies, a baseball game, or church. Anywhere with rows of seats was off-limits. Sadly, because of their behaviors many such students have no social, spiritual, or recreational activities in the community. The entire responsibility falls on the family members.

In a literature review, Horner, Carr, Strain, Todd & Reed (2002) found that children with autism are at a significant risk to develop inappropriate behaviors including self-injury, destruction of property, and physical aggression. Without appropriate interventions the behaviors may become worse, and they have a major impact on the person's opportunities to live in the community.

Early and sustained interventions to minimize inappropriate behaviors are essential. Meta-analyses, reviews of the literature, and reports of interventions for children with ASD have demonstrated that evidence-based behavioral interventions hold the best promise of being effective in diminishing many of the troublesome behaviors.

UNDERSTANDING THE INDIVIDUAL

The critical first step in diminishing inappropriate behavior is a complete understanding of the individual's characteristics and circumstances. The failure of most consequence-based behavior management based on rewards and punishments is often due to the cognitive style and perceptions of the individual, not that they are "spoiled" or "getting away with it."

OBSESSIVE-COMPULSIVE BEHAVIORS

Many individuals with ASD display obsessive-compulsive behaviors. These were first identified by Asperger in 1991. Usually the obsessive behaviors are an intense interest in a specific subject or thing. Many children with ASD become fervently interested in trains, for example. They want to look at pictures of them, read stories about them, line toy train cars up in a specific order, and if verbal, talk only about trains. Others are obsessed with maps or public transportation timetables.

One child with ASD knew the address of every single child and teacher in the school. Unfortunately, when he got angry at someone he would recite their address. Teachers and other students found this distressing. Another child always spent recess at the outside perimeter of the playground. He never interacted with any other child or adult, but stood at the edge of the fence. The teachers assumed he was frightened by the noise and commotion on the playground. However, it is always critical to observe each child very carefully. A closer observation of this young boy revealed that he was imitating birdcalls. He had taught himself to make an exact imitation of over 20 different calls including blue jays, tufted tit-mice, crows, and even the rose-breasted grosbeak!

Limiting a student's ability to perseverate on their obsession can result in aggressive behaviors such as kicking, spitting, grabbing, or screaming. These children have learned that these behaviors will result in the obsessive object being allowed. Teachers and families struggle with what to do about compulsive behaviors. Should they be allowed or disrupted? How can these behaviors be minimized? We will learn that rewarding a compulsion is not recommended.

PERFECTIONISM

In addition to rigid thinking about certain things, many students with ASD have a tendency toward perfection. They may become extremely distressed when things do not follow a specific pattern or schedule. They can be upset for long periods when the school day is changed due to inclement weather or a special occasion. Fire drills and other surprises can engender outbursts of screaming or crying. These students crave a situation in which everything is predictable. From their perspective, things should follow a specific pattern in a rigid and unchanging way.

Mistakes, like changes, can also be quite distressing for students with ASD. Some students have a tendency toward perfectionism, and not getting everything correct can be a source of extreme stress. Shakeem erased holes in his papers trying to get every single letter he wrote perfectly formed.

Stress has been shown to be very difficult for those with ASD. When individuals are stressed, by a fire drill, for example, the body produces cortisol, a neurobiological stress hormone reflecting hypothalamic-pituitary-adrenal (HPA) axis activity. Cortisol is secreted by the adrenal glands. It has been termed the stress hormone because it is secreted at higher levels during the flight-or-fight response to stress. Small increases have positive effects; however, higher levels have been shown to impact cognitive function. We feel agitated, and depending on the level of cortisol, may temporarily lose the ability to access higher-order thinking skills.

According to the research of Corbett, Swain, Newsom, Wang, Song & Edgerton (2014), there is a spectrum of responsivity to stress. Some typically developing individuals have high levels of cortisol when faced with a stressful situation, while others have abnormally low levels (Ruttle, Shirtcliff, Serbin, Fisher, Stack & Schwartzman, 2011). The length of time the stress arousal persists is also relative to the level of cortisol.

Individuals like Michael typically have hyper-responsivity to stress (Corbett, Schupp & Lanni, 2012). When an individual with ASD is faced with an unexpected situation, say, a mistake or the absence of a favored object, the event may present as much more stressful to them than to typically developing individuals. Their cortisol levels remain high for an extended period.

Physiologically, Michael was simply unable to calm down at the baseball game, even though he wanted very much to stay. Spratt et al. (2011) found significantly higher serum cortisol response in a group of children with autism. Analysis showed significantly higher peak cortisol levels and prolonged duration of the cortisol elevation in children with autism.

Michael's brain was flooded with cortisol, and he could not process his family's reassurance that it was okay to be a little late to a baseball game. It is not that he would not listen to logic, his brain was so chemically stressed from rushing and his need for a perfect schedule that he could not respond as he would normally. His parents were also stressed about being late but were able to calm down in a little while. After this episode, he was upset for the entire weekend.

GENERALIZATION

Lack of generalization across different settings is a common characteristic of students with ASD and those with other developmental disabilities. This is most likely due to their rigid thought process. They tend to be black and white in their thinking. There is no in-between. They exhibit what is called "overselective responding" by Koegel (1995). This means that they associate everything they learn with very specific conditions. They may learn to say hello to the teacher and aide and hang up their coat upon entering the classroom, but fail to do this in any other place or situation. This can be very upsetting to families who hear how well their child is doing at school when they fail to see at home any of the behaviors being described.

COMMUNICATION

Individuals with ASD and those with developmental disabilities frequently have difficulties with communication. They may be nonverbal or have limited verbal expressive skills. Often, problem behaviors are due to communication deficits (Iovannone et al., 2003).

Students who do not speak may learn to use inappropriate behaviors to communicate their wants and needs. For example, they may push papers to the floor or refuse to look at an item, scream or spit when they want the teacher to leave them alone.

STRENGTHS

No discussion of the characteristics of individuals with ASD and developmental disabilities should ever occur without a consideration of their strengths. Many individuals with Down syndrome are cheerful and loving. They are highly attuned to the feelings of others and are a joy in many classrooms and families.

Individuals with ASD have transformed our world. Temple Grandin made animal slaughterhouses more humane, and Allan Speerling invented the computer. Steve Jobs, Einstein, and many others have been posthumously diagnosed with ASD. Many of the techniques teachers have learned by working with disabled students have been effective with other students as well.

FUNCTIONAL BEHAVIOR ASSESSMENT

A developmental history, an assessment of the current environment, and a careful description of the individual's appropriate and inappropriate behaviors are the foundation of intervention. We begin with the assumption that all behavior serves a function. Once the function of the behavior is determined we can employ targeted strategies that will better enable the individual to meet their needs in a more positive manner.

Functional behavior assessment (FBA) is an individualized process. It is used in an attempt to discern the purpose or function of a child's behavior. Difficult behaviors are often a way for a person with developmental disabilities to make their needs and wishes known (Mildon, Moore & Dixon, 2004). A student might bite himself to avoid a task or to gain attention. These children have learned that such behaviors get results. In order to change the behavior, we must understand the purpose that maintains it.

The best way to discover the function of behaviors is to conduct a functional assessment. This is a term that includes both direct and indirect observations of the child to understand why the child engages in a problem behavior. When we have a good idea about why a child uses a behavior, we are in a much better position to develop effective interventions that will allow a child to meet their needs in a more socially acceptable way.

An FBA begins with agreement by teachers, parents, and specialists on the selection of a behavior that should be diminished. Objectively describing the behavior is one of the most important steps. Through careful observations the behavior is described operationally, including when it is most likely to occur. Amazingly, this is one of the most difficult tasks. We often speak of "disruptive" students, or students who have "temper tantrums." These are not helpful terms. They can mean different things to different people. How would you describe a temper tantrum? Hitting? Spitting? Throwing papers? Throwing books or chairs? Throwing a paper on the floor is very different from throwing a chair.

In order to change or diminish challenging behavior, we must first define it operationally. The behavior must be described so that anyone who observes the student can see whether or not the behavior occurs. They must be able to observe it quickly and without question. The behavior must be defined so that anyone could count the number of times it happens or the length or duration of the behavior.

These cannot be abstract judgments, such as: "she is a difficult student," "she is hard to manage," or "she is disruptive." They must be concrete, observable behaviors. Some examples can be: "she takes materials from other students and knocks things off desks," "she bites the outside skin on her left wrist hard enough to leave teeth marks," or "he makes about one shrill shriek a second long that is loud enough to be heard in the hallway!"

Simon's teachers wanted to develop a plan to stop him from hitting. It seemed like he was constantly hitting everyone all day. His teachers were exhausted and had tried every consequence they could think of including time out, loss of points, isolation, and

Change these general descriptions into concrete observable behaviors. When are these behaviors most likely to occur?

BEHAVIOR	WHEN?
He screams	
She hurts others	
He kicks	
He won't sit still	
She is a runner	
He spits	
She grabs things	
He gets upset when the schedule is changed	

Figure 4.1. Managing your own behavior. *Source: Jeanne D'Haem*

sending him home. Nothing worked, and it seemed like the hitting was only getting worse.

First, the team needed to objectively describe the target behavior, hitting. They needed to determine how Simon hit, when he hit, and who he hit. With this information they would have a better chance of determining why he hit, or the function of this behavior. Close observations revealed that Simon hit a person's back with the open palm of his hand. He never used a closed fist, never slapped a person's face, or grabbed. He simply hit one time in the middle of a person's back. Observations during several activities showed that he only hit people he liked: his aide, the teacher, and two of the girls in the classroom. He never hit the boys and typically stayed away from them. The hitting occurred most often during a work session when he had been working for five minutes on an academic task.

INFORMATION GATHERING

Once an operational definition of the behavior has been agreed upon, a careful study of the person is required. Indirect strategies include interviews with people who work with the student, family members, and the person themselves, whenever possible. The functional assessment interview (FAI) or The Student Guided Functional Assessment Interview (O'Neill et al., 1997) might be used when the students can be asked to provide information. Behavioral rating scales can also be helpful. The Motivation Assessment Scale (MAS) (Durand & Crimmins, 1992) and the Functional Analysis Screening Tool (FAST) (Iwata & DeLeon, 1996) were developed to determine the likely maintaining function of a behavior.

The purpose of this information is to gather as complete a picture as possible of the events and the environment in which the problem behavior is most likely to occur. How old are they? What is their ability level in self-help, communication, academics, and social skills? What factors from the home and school influence the behavior? How large is the family? How many other students are in the classroom? What interventions have been tried before? Most importantly, what are this child's likes and dislikes? Do they have a primary obsession? Is there a secondary obsession?

In Simon's case, the team was surprised to note that he only hit people he liked. He did not appear angry, and he always hit with an open palm, not a fist or a poke. His teachers thought he might be looking for attention. His background clearly showed that he could easily learn new hand motions even though he did not speak. Based on this information they taught him to hold up his hand to ask for a "high five." Simon loved this new skill and quickly learned to ask for a high five instead of hitting his teacher on the back.

Functional behavior assessment is a process to determine why and when a problem behavior occurs. As you know, Billy would grab onto a person's hair and not let go. Several times he pulled handfuls of hair out of the scalp. A functional behavior assessment can help to determine what happens just before the hair pulling occurs and what happens during and after the episode that increases the probability of future occurrences.

Once the background information is collected and the behavior has been defined so that any person who observed that behavior would agree that it had occurred, a series of baseline observations are made. Antecedent conditions that prompt the behavior as well as the maintaining consequences are studied. This information is analyzed to determine a hypothesis. For example, a careful analysis of Billy's day revealed that any time the slightest thing changed, he showed signs of anxiety and might reach for his teacher's hair. This behavior was maintained by attention from male staff members who intervened. Billy seemed to like them and would often try to get their attention by grabbing.

Once the function of the behavior is identified, interventions based on this understanding have a higher probability of success.

This is critical because some interventions may actually increase the use of inappropriate behavior. Others work so slowly that teachers may give up before they realize the interventions are effective. Once the intent is known, students may be taught a better way to meet their objective. This new behavior is known as the replacement behavior.

Billy's teachers knew that he needed a very strict schedule that could not be varied, even by a few minutes. They learned to watch for signs of anxiety. He would bite his bottom lip when he started to become anxious. When he did grab, he could be distracted by a loud noise instead of physical contact by the male classroom aides. His teachers also discovered that he was more likely to obey a request to let go if it came from a puppet rather than a live person.

DATA COLLECTION FROM OBSERVATIONS OF THE BEHAVIOR

ABC Analysis

There are several procedures that can give a baseline of the behavior. The choice of instrument depends on the behavior that the student displays. Infrequent episodic behaviors may be observed using an ABC Descriptive Analysis. This provides a structure where the behavior can be noted along with the environmental events that precede and follow the behavior. A = antecedent. What was happening just before the behavior occurred? B = behavior. The objectively stated behavior or cluster of behaviors during an event, such as a tantrum. C = consequence. What was the immediate consequence of the behavior? These may include events or reactions of the teachers or other students.

Scatter Plot Analysis

The scatter plot can be used to record behaviors that are frequent and finite such as hitting or screaming. A grid is prepared where observation periods are plotted along the horizontal line and time is plotted along the vertical line. Each cell contains an indication if the behavior occurred at a high rate, low rate, or not at all. Numbers can be used to document how often the behavior is seen. A pattern, if one exists, will emerge after several days of plotting. A scatter plot can indicate that a behavior correlates to a time of day, certain people, activities, or the physical environment.

ANALYSIS AND BEHAVIOR INTERVENTION PLAN

Once the functional assessment is complete, the data is analyzed to determine the maintaining function of the behavior. Function-based interventions are designed, including teaching the replacement behavior if necessary. Antecedent adjustments are made to prompt the replacement behavior. Reinforcements are offered for the replacement behavior and extinction of the target behavior (Lane, Cook & Tankersley 2013).

EVIDENCE-BASED INTERVENTIONS

Meta-analyses, reviews of the literature, and reports of interventions for children with ASD have demonstrated that evidence-based behavioral interventions are an effective intervention for this population. The National Autism Center (NAC) and the National Professional Development Center on ASD (NPDC) have been instrumental in determining evidence-based practices for students with ASD. Enough high-quality studies were published in refereed journals to support a conclusion that they produced beneficial outcomes. Intervention outcomes include a decrease in problem behaviors, a reduction in repetitive behaviors, and improved sensory/emotional regulation.

The National Autism Center's National Standards Report (NAC, 2009) identified 11 established treatments in their review of evidence-based treatments, all of which involved behavioral procedures in some capacity. The New York State Department of Health (NYSDOH, 1999) identified early behavioral interventions as an evidence-based treatment for children with ASD up to the age of three years in their clinical practice guideline report. Moreover, meta-analyses with effect-size calculations have provided further support for using behavioral interventions with children with ASD. Eldevik et al. (2009) evaluated studies using group designs and demonstrated that early intensive behavioral intervention is effective in increasing cognitive and adaptive functioning.

NAC-ESTABLISHED INTERVENTIONS

- Antecedent strategies: Precede target behaviors, and include behavior chain interruptions, choice, priming, non-contingent reinforcement, environmental modification
- Behavioral interventions: Uses behavior change including mand or ABA training, discrete trial teaching, differential reinforcement strategies, token economy
- Behavioral treatment for young children: Combination of ABA discrete trial and incidental teaching
- Joint action: Teaching child to respond to nonverbal social cues
- Modeling: Adults give demonstration of behavior for imitation, including video modeling
- Naturalistic teaching: Adult follows the child's lead and interests
- Peer training: Circle of friends, integrated play groups
- Pivotal response: Targets behavior that influences other areas, including self-management
- Schedules

- Self-management: Behavior regulation through reinforcement. Checklists, wrist counters, visual prompts, tokens
- Social stories: Provides information on who/what/why/when of target behavior

Due to the difficulties in effecting changes in the behavior of individuals with ASD, it is imperative that the NAC interventions are tried first. Some interventions actually increase inappropriate behaviors and then make the behavior even more difficult to extinguish. Progress is often slow, and valuable time may be wasted on poor interventions. For example, facilitated communication and the gluten- and casein-free diet were not effective. The NAC's recommendation for educators is to give consideration first to research-based treatments. Teachers should consider unestablished treatments only after some level of effectiveness has been published in a refereed journal. It is important to remember that treatment selection is quite complicated, and the student's unique characteristics must be considered along with family preferences. Most importantly, treatment decisions must be based on data.

Procedures that yield, on average, medium-to-strong effect sizes include behavioral skills training, prompting procedures, differential reinforcement, and video modeling. Effect sizes ranging from 91.35 to 93.37 suggest minimal differences between these interventions.

ANTECEDENT MANAGEMENT

Antecedent interventions are based on preventing problem behaviors. Many teachers and families try to change behavior by using a negative consequence after the behavior occurs. This is often ineffective for students with ASD because the more they engage in a behavior the more likely they are to repeat it. A far more effective technique is to identify the behavioral trigger and alter it, teach replacement behaviors that are incompatible with the challenging behavior, and use reinforcements to increase appropriate behaviors (Marks et al., 2006). Some individuals benefit from intervention strategies related to sensory regulation and stimulation. Other strategies promote generalization and maintenance of behavior and prevent recurrence of challenging behaviors.

The more common antecedent interventions are behavioral skills training, including differential reinforcement, video modeling, mindfulness exercises, social story task analyses, prompting, and role-playing. These are considered the most representative of a set of procedures that yield, on average, medium-to-strong effect sizes.

Differential Reinforcement of Behavior

Since consequence strategies are frequently ineffective with students with ASD, a more effective approach is to increase the occurrence of appropriate behavior. Differential reinforcement of other behavior (DRO) refers to giving reinforcement after a child has not exhibited a target behavior during a set interval of time.

For example, Marci could earn time on the iPad for staying in her seat for 15 minutes. The initial DRO schedule should be related to the original rate of behavior. If a child was shrieking an average of 10 times in a 60-minute period, then reinforcement for not shrieking should be given every six minutes (Repp, Felce & Barton, 1991). There are many ways that a DRO can be modified based on the specific situation and behavior.

Reinforcement can be offered if a child is not displaying the target behavior at a preselected time. The interval can be reset each time the target behavior occurs. Eric was rewarded with a small cracker when he did not bite his wrist for 10 minutes. Each time he bit his wrist, the 10-minute interval would reset. If an interval began at 10 but he bit his wrist at 10:05, a new 10-minute interval would begin.

Differential reinforcement of incompatible behaviors (DRI) can be used when there is a behavior that is topographically incompatible with the inappropriate behavior. Donald was obsessed with light switches. He liked to flip them off and on and would even walk into other classrooms to do so. His teacher rewarded him for keeping his hands in his pockets any time he walked around the classroom or in the hall. It was impossible for him to play with a light switch when his hands were in his pockets. Eric was rewarded for having his hands in his lap. He could not bite his wrist if his hands were in his lap.

A critical and often overlooked element in any DRO schedule is fading. Realistically it is difficult for a teacher to consistently follow a DRO schedule for extended periods. Some students figure out the DRO and will increase other inappropriate behaviors, or even learn to exhibit the target in order to reset the interval. Most importantly, the goal is always for the student to behave appropriately in response to natural reinforcements.

VIDEO AND PICTURE INTERVENTIONS

Video-based interventions (including picture icons, video modeling, and video prompting) yield a medium effect indicating an effective intervention. The use of video-based interventions has increased in the past decade, and the results of the current meta-analysis and other analyses seem to support the use of these interventions for individuals with ASD across their lifespan.

For students with developmental disabilities and ASD, problem behaviors are often due to difficulties with communication (Iovannone et al., 2003). A child with ASD often resorts to inappropriate behavior to communicate wants and needs. Jason punched his teacher on her back when he wanted to get some praise and a break from working. Functional communication training (FCT) involves assessing the function of the behavior then teaching the child a better way to communicate wants. Often pictures are used that depict different outcomes. A child can be taught to point to the correct picture to indicate what is desired.

Research has found that students with ASD can learn skills by watching videos that model appropriate behaviors. Typically in this intervention, individuals watch a video presenting the behavior then are asked to imitate it. VSM or video self-modeling is an application where individuals observe themselves successfully performing a behavior (Bellini & Akullian, 2007).

MINDFULNESS EXERCISES

Breathing is an important tool for calming the mind. Inhaling and exhaling slowly helps the body become calm. Individuals with ASD can be taught slow, careful breathing techniques. Directing a person to "breathe with me" is much more effective than shouting "calm down!"

Prompting and Role-Playing

Robin, Schneider & Dolnick (1976) developed a technique to teach children how to manage aggressive impulses when they are upset. It is called the turtle technique. Children are taught to pull their arms and legs close to their bodies and role-play or pretend they are a turtle drawing into their shell. They stay in this position long enough to take three to five long, deep breaths. Once the technique has been taught, students can be prompted to assume this position, which can be quite soothing to an overstimulated child.

INTERVENTIONS FOR PHYSICAL AGITATION

Physical Restraint

There are two categories of physical restraint: manual and mechanical. Manual restraint is when a teacher or other caregiver restrains a student. Mechanical restraint involves an apparatus such as straps or blankets. There are many, many problems with restraint. Without proper assessment of environmental and antecedent factors, restraint can serve as reinforcement for antisocial behavior (Magee & Ellis, 2001). It does not promote the acquisition of better skills, and the physical contact may actually reinforce the dangerous behavior.

Furthermore, restraint may serve as reinforcement for staff members who are rewarded with the cessation of the behavior and admiration from other staff members (Jones & Timbers, 2002). Restraint draws attention to the individual and is potentially dangerous. Restraint should only be used as a temporary measure and never as a planned consequence for inappropriate behaviors. In an emergency, only those who have been trained in the proper and safe use of restraints should participate.

Individuals with ASD are physiologically prone to higher levels of cortical excitation than others. Caregivers, teachers, and parents must be aware of this chemical response to stress and its longer duration. Most people know when they are getting upset and have developed strategies to help them calm down. This is even more important for children and adults with autism. Understanding that adrenal cortical excitation can last for hours, or even days in some individuals, is crucial when designing interventions.

Typical descriptions of the student include "went crazy," "lost it," and "gone nuts." These descriptions are harmful because they blame the person and do not acknowledge the cortisol excitation that has made them biologically unable to access normal thinking. We would not punish a person with cerebral palsy for walking slowly. It is well established that people with ASD easily become overaroused, and once overstimulated, they remain so for extended periods (Baranek, 2002). Individuals with ASD, in a state of adrenal cortisol arousal, are not able to respond appropriately. It is impossible for them to do so!

Once we understand what is happening physically to individuals with autism when they are stressed, it becomes clear that having appropriate interventions in place is crucial. Walker et al. (1995) conceptualized the "acting out cycle." The phases of calm, agitation, out-of-control, de-escalation, and recovery are widely accepted. Occasionally we do not know what has triggered the agitation, since there are both fast and slow triggers. A person may become upset by a loud noise, or a series of small events such as their favorite shirt not being available and the bus running late. During this period, stressed individuals are unable to stay on task and may be noncompliant. Confrontation or punishment at this stage may serve as an additional trigger and result in an even greater adrenal cortisol secretion.

During the acceleration phase, many individuals will attempt to draw others in by hitting or screaming. In peak out-of-control periods, cortisol has impaired cognitive function. Restraint is sometimes needed in order to keep the person from harming themselves or others. During the de-escalation period, students become calmer. Finally the cortisol level diminishes and a period of subdued behavior and interactions follows.

The response to a student who is agitated or even in the out-of-control phase is critical. Punishment will only increase the stress reaction. There should be consequences for inappropriate behaviors; however, during the throes of an episode is not the time to enforce them. A person in the midst of adrenal cortical excitation is not capable of learning, so response strategies need to be taught and reviewed frequently before an event occurs.

Individuals have different ways to recover from stressful situations. When parents, teachers, or caregivers are aware of individual preferences, they can offer choices. Music can be very calming. Some teachers use motor-related songs, beginning with large movements and ending with whispers and slow, controlled movements. Backrubs, beanbag chairs, or slow rocking can be soothing and allow the brain to quiet down. The old phrase "take a walk and get a drink" is often effective since water can help to dilute the cortisol.

SOCIAL STORIES

Social stories, developed by Carol Gray (in 1993), are antecedent prompts to prepare individuals with ASD for events that are stressful to them. They describe situations from the person's point of view and suggest different behaviors. Once a trigger has been identified, a story can be written to prepare the individual with a way to manage the stressful stimulus.

Nathan hated loud noises, especially fire drills. He would scream for hours after the loud warning rang. So we wrote *The Fire Drill Social Story* with him. The book acknowledged his stress, and related a sequence of events he should follow. He read the book over and over on fire drill days and was able to keep himself calmer, refraining from screaming. The social story must be written based on the individual circumstances of the child due to their frequent difficulties with generalization.

David became agitated and would scream and lash out at others if his bus was late or the daily schedule changed. Sending him to a "time-out" room, as punishment for screaming and biting, increased his behavior. A calm-down area was created in a private corner. David was introduced to the area when he was calm. He was taught that he could choose to listen to music, look at train schedules, or sit in the beanbag chair. He found the beanbag chair soothing and would often pull a second one on top during highly stressful times, similar to Temple Grandin's squeeze machine. His teachers would gently lead him to the calm-down area when he exhibited early signs of agitation. Careful observations demonstrated that he would begin by avoiding eye contact and emit shrill, frequent squeaks, which quickly turned into screams and flailing at anyone who approached. His teachers would point to the calm-down area and guide him to it. He was usually able to return to his task after about 20 minutes. Eventually he learned to mand for or request the calm-down area.

Aversive Stimuli

The use of aversive stimuli results in the student experiencing physical pain or discomfort. Some aversives are natural. Touching a hot pot will produce a change in behavior without any previous learning. Mild aversives include water, lemon juice and ammonia, and physical restraint. For example, a fine mist of water is sprayed toward a person exhibiting inappropriate behaviors.

Kelly did not like loud noises, and she especially disliked the sound of a balloon popping. When she began to engage in disruptive behavior by throwing objects around the room, her teacher would get out a balloon and blow it up. She would stop the behavior when she saw the balloon. Eventually, her teacher did not need to blow up the balloon but merely take it out of her desk. Finally a picture of a balloon would stop the throwing.

The potentially harmful nature of aversives requires careful employment.

1. Application must be determined by a team of professionals, including the family.
2. It must be based on a functional assessment.
3. All staff must be carefully trained.
4. It must be in accordance with school and legal guidelines.

There are many problems with the use of aversives. The student may strike back, become withdrawn and tune out, or the student may engage in escape and avoidance behaviors (Alberto & Troutman 2006).

When a student displays severe or persistent behavioral issues, two people are involved. The student and you (i.e., the teacher, parent, or other caregiver)! Managing behavior is very difficult both physically and emotionally. When caregivers are stressed because a student is spitting at them or grabbing their hair, they are producing cortisol as well as the student. Cortisol, the neurobiological stress hormone, is automatically secreted by the adrenal glands and we do not control it. Teachers, parents, and even police officers often feel agitated when confronted with a difficult person. Depending on the level of cortisol, they may temporarily lose the ability to access their rational thinking skills and remain professional during an altercation. It is critical for teachers and other caregivers to take good care of themselves. An upset person is not helpful.

Superman and Wonder Woman Are Not Real!

1. List what happens when you are getting stressed:

   • Shortened breath
   • Sweaty palms
   • Red face
   • _____

2. In classrooms where students have inappropriate behaviors, teachers must have a signal to alert others that they are feeling stressed and need to remove themselves from the situation. This can take 10–20 minutes. What signals do you use in your classroom or with your family?

3. Make a list of activities that help you calm down:

   • Quiet time away from the situation
   • Talking to someone
   • Movement such as walking, push-ups
   • Music

- Food, drink
- _____
- _____

I hearby give permission for teachers and family members to admit they are sometimes stressed by inappropriate behaviors. Talk to an aide, family member, neighbor, or another teacher about your stress. Discuss how they can assist and take over for 15–20 minutes until the feelings diminish. Give yourself a few minutes of soothing time several times each day. Breathe deeply at stoplights, stay in the car for a few minutes when you get home and take a three-minute "vacation." A calm, well-rested teacher is an effective teacher.

ALTERNATIVE AND MEDICAL INTERVENTIONS

Research has not found evidence of the efficacy of many interventions, including facilitated communication, auditory integration training, secretin, dietary interventions, chelation, and dolphin-assisted therapy.

Psychotropic medications can be an important element in a treatment plan for individuals with ASD. Behaviors such as aggression, self-injurious behaviors, obsessions that restrict activities of daily living, and dangerous impulsive behaviors such as mouthing or eating inappropriate items may warrant medical interventions (Broun & Umbarger, 2005). Medications are most effective when they are part of a treatment plan that includes behavioral strategies, family education, and special education services (Hendren & Martin, 2005).

The only medications currently approved for ASD by the U.S. Food and Drug Administration are Risperal and Abilify. They are approved only for irritability in 5–16-year-olds with ASD. Side effects include weight gain and sedation. Any drug used to improve

Jeanne D'Haem

mood or behavior should only be used with a team that coordinates treatment and care. Outcomes must be tracked and used in ongoing reviews of the person's behavior, and the lowest dose possible must be used.

SUMMARY

This chapter discussed behavioral excesses such as self-stimulation, resistance to change, aggressive behaviors, and self-injurious actions of students with ASD and other developmental disorders. Without interventions to diminish these behaviors, these individuals face significant impairment in the areas of independent living, employment, and social and romantic relationships.

The critical first step in decreasing inappropriate behavior is a complete understanding of the individual's characteristics and circumstances. A developmental history, an assessment of the environment, and a careful description of the individual's behaviors are the foundation of intervention. Infrequent episodic behaviors may be observed using an ABC Descriptive Analysis. Scatter Plot Analysis can be used to record behaviors that are frequent and finite such as hitting or screaming.

Once the function of the behavior is determined, evidence-based interventions can be used. These include behavioral skills training, prompting procedures, differential reinforcement of other behavior, and video modeling.

Occasionally manual or mechanical physical restraint must be used. However, there are many problems with restraint. The use of aversive stimuli that results in physical pain or discomfort to the student is also problematic. Psychotropic medications can be an important element in a treatment plan for individuals with ASD who exhibit behaviors such as aggression, self-injurious behaviors, and dangerous impulsive behaviors. Medications are most effective when they are part of a treatment plan that includes behavioral strategies, family education, and special education services.

REFERENCES

Alberto, P. A., & Troutman, A. C. (2006). *Applied Behavior Analysis for teachers*. Upper Saddle River, NJ: Pearson.

Asperger, H. (1991). Autistic psychopathy in childhood. In U. Firth (Ed.), *Autism and Asperger syndrome* (pp. 37–92). New York: Cambridge University Press.

Bambara, I. M., Nonnemacher, S., & Kern, L. (2009). Sustaining school-based individualized positive behavior support. *Journal of Positive Behavior Interventions, 11*(3), 161–76.

Baranek, G. (2002). Efficacy of sensory and motor interventions for children with autism. *Journal of Autism and Developmental Disorders, 32*(5), 397–422.

Bellini, S., & Akullian, J. (2007). A meta-analysis on video modeling and video self-modeling interventions for children with autism spectrum disorder. *Exceptional Children, 73*(3), 264–87.

Belvel, P. S., & Jordan, M. M. (2003). *Rethinking classroom management: Strategies for prevention, intervention, and problem solving*. Thousand Oaks, CA: Corwin Press.

Broun, L. & Umbarger, G. (2005). Considerations on the use of medications with people who have autism spectrum disorder. Position paper, Division on Developmental Disabilities.

Canter, L., & Canter, M. (2001). *Assertive discipline: Positive behavior management for today's classroom*. Los Angeles: Canter and Associates.

Chandler, L. K., & Dahlquist, C. M. (2002). *Functional assessment: Strategies to prevent and remediate challenging behavior in school settings*. Upper Saddle River, NJ: Merrill Prentice Hall.

Charles, C. M. (2002). *Essential elements of effective discipline*. Boston: Allyn & Bacon.

Corbett, B. A., Schupp, C. W., & Lanni, K. E. (2012). Comparing biobehavioral profiles across two social stress paradigms in children with and without autism spectrum disorders. *Molecular Autism, 3*(13),1–10.

Corbett, B. A., Swain, D. M., Newsom, C., Wang, L., Song, Y., & Edgerton, D. (2014). Biobehavioral profiles of arousal and social motivation in autism spectrum disorders. *Journal of Child Psychology and Psychiatry, 55*(8), 924–34.

Danforth, S., & Boyle, J. R. (2000). *Cases in behavior management*. Upper Saddle River, NJ: Prentice Hall.

Durand, V., & Crimmins, D. (1992). *The Motivation Assessment Scale* (MAS). Topeka, KS: Monaco & Associates, Inc.

Eldevik, S., Hastings, R., Hughes, J. (2009). Meta-analysis of Early Intensive Behavioral Intervention for children with autism. *Journal of Clinical Child and Adolescent Psychology, 38*(3), 439–50. doi: 10.1080/ 15374410902851739.

Forness, S. R., Walker, H. M., & Kavale, K. A. (2003). Psychiatric disorders and treatment: a primer for teachers. *Teaching Exceptional Children, 36*(2), 42–49.

Friend, M., & Bursuck, W. D. (2002). *Including students with special needs: A practical guide for classroom teachers.* Boston: Allyn & Bacon.

Graetz, J. E., Mastropieri, M. A., & Scruggs, T. E. (2009). Decreasing inappropriate behaviors for adolescents with autism spectrum disorders using modified social stories. *Education and Training in Developmental Disabilities, 44*(1), 91–104.

Gray, C. (1994). *The new social stories book.* Los Angeles: Future Directions.

Hagerty, N. K., Black, R. S., & Smith, G. J. (2005). Increasing self-managed coping skills through social stories and apron storytelling. *Teaching Exceptional Children, 37*(4), 40–47.

Hendren, R., & Martin, A. (2005). Pharmacotherapy. In L. J. Baker & L. A. Welkowitz (Eds.), *Asperger's Syndrome: Intervening in Schools, Clinics, and Communities* (63–81). Mahwah, NJ: Lawrence Erlbaum.

Horner, R. H., Carr, E. G., Strain, P. S., Todd, A. W., & Reed, H. K. (2002). Problem behavior interventions for young children with autism: A research synthesis. *Journal of Autism and Developmental Disorders, 32*: 423–46.

Iovannone, R., Dunlap, G., Huber, H., & Kincaid, D. (2003). Effective educational practices for students with autism spectrum disorders. *Focus on Autism and Other Developmental Disabilities, 18*: 150–65.

Iwata, B., & DeLeon, I. (1996). *The functional analysis screening tool.* The Florida Center on Self-Injury. Gainesville: University of Florida.

Jacobs, W., and Nadel, L. (1985). Stress-induced recovery of fears and phobias. *Psychological Review, 92*(4), 512–31.

Jones, R. J., & Timbers, G. D. (2002). An analysis of the restraint event and its behavioral effects on clients and staff. *Reclaiming Children and Youth, 11*(37), 41.

Koegel, R. L. & Koegel, L. K. (1995). Teaching children with autism: Strategies for initiating positive interactions and improving learning opportunities. Baltimore: P. H. Brookes Pub. Co.

Kuhn, D. E., Hardesty, S. L., & Sweeney, N. M. (2009). Assessment and treatment of excessive straightening and destructive behavior in an adolescent diagnosed with autism. *Journal of Applied Behavior Analysis, 42*(2), 355–60. doi:10.1901/jaba.2009.42-355.

Lane, L. L., Cook, B. G., & Tankersley, M. (2013). *Research-based strategies for improving outcomes in behavior.* Boston: Pearson Education, Inc.

Magee, S. K., & Ellis, J. (2001). The detrimental effects of physical restraint as a consequence for inappropriate classroom behavior. *Journal of Applied Behavior Analysis, 34*: 501–04.

Marks, S. U., Hudson, J., Schrader, C., Longaker, T., & Levine, M. (2006). Reconsidering behavior management for students with autism spectrum disorders. *Beyond Behavior, 15*(2), 7–12.

Martella, R., Nelson, J., & Marchand-Martella, N. (2003). *Managing disruptive behaviors in the schools.* Boston: Pearson Education, Inc.

Maurice, C. (1993). *Let me hear your voice: A family's triumph over autism.* New York: Fawcett Books.

Mildon, R. L., Moore, D. W., & Dixon, R. S. (2004). Combining noncontingent escape and functional communication training as a treatment for negatively reinforced disruptive behavior. *Journal of Positive Behavior Interventions, 6,* 92–102.

O'Neill, R., Horner, R., Albin, R., Sprague, J., Storey, K., & Newton, J. (1997). *Functional assessment and program development for problem behavior,* 2nd ed. Pacific Grove, CA: Brooks/Cole Publishing Co.

Repp, A. C., Felce, D., & Barton, L. E. (1991). The effects of initial interval size of the efficacy of DRO schedules of reinforcement. *Exceptional Children, 57*: 417–25.

Robin, A., Schneider, M., & Dolnick, M. (1976). The turtle technique: An extended case study of self-control in the classroom. *Psychology in the Schools, 12*: 120–28.

Ruttle, P. L., Shirtcliff, E. A., Serbin, L. A., Fisher, D. B., Stack, D. M., & Schwartzman, A. E. (2011). Disentangling psychobiological mechanisms underlying internalizing and externalizing behaviors in youth: Longitudinal and concurrent associations with cortisol. *Hormones and Behavior, 59*: 123–32.

Ryan, A. L., Halsey, H. N., & Matthews, W. J. (2003). Using functional assessment to promote desirable student behavior in schools. *Teaching Exceptional Children, 35*(5), 8–15.

Scheuerman, B. & Webber, J. (2002). *Autism: Teaching DOES make a difference.* Belmont, CA: Wadsworth-Thompson Learning.

Singh, N. N., Lancioni, G. E., Manikam, R., Winton, A. S. W., Singh, A. N. A., Singh, J., et al. (2011a). A mindfulness-based strategy for self-management of aggressive behavior in adolescents with autism. *Research in Autism Spectrum Disorders, 5*(3), 1153–58. doi: 10.1016/j.rasd.2010.12.012 .

Singh, N. N., Lancioni, G. E., Singh, A. D. A., Winton, A. S. W., Singh, A. N. A., & Singh, J. (2011b). Adolescents with Asperger's syndrome can use a mindfulness-based strategy to control their aggressive behavior. *Research in Autism Spectrum Disorders , 5* (3), 1103–09. doi: 10.1016/j.rasd.2010.12.006 .

Spratt, J., Nicholas, J., Brady, K., Carpenter, L., Hatcher, C., Meekins, K., Furlanetto, R., & Charles, J. (2011). Enhanced cortisol response to stress in children in autism. *Journal of Autism and Developmental Disorders.* doi: 10.1007/ s108033-011—1214-0 75-81.

Sugai, G. (2009). *School-wide positive behavior support and response to interventions.* Washington, DC: Office of Special Education Programs, U.S. Department of Education.

Walker, M., Calvin, G., & Ramsey, D. (1995). *Antisocial behavior in schools: Strategies and best practices.* Pacific Grove, CA: Brooks/Cole Publishing.

WEBSITES:

Classroom Management Topics Index: http://www.helpguide.ord/harvard/autism-behavior-problems.htm.

Chapter Five

Language Development and AAC for Students with ASD/SD

Pei-Lin Weng

Communication is a vital skill. Human beings use many different means of communication, such as sounds, facial expressions, gestures, sign language, and speech, to convey their needs and wants. For example, newborns use crying to communicate a need such as feeding; toddlers use gestures and words to request toys; teenagers use text and speech to socialize with peers. In this chapter, we will first discuss the characteristics of language development and communication in individuals with autism spectrum disorder (ASD) and/or severe disability (SD). We will then focus a great deal on augmentative and alternative communication (AAC) from the following angles: what AAC is, types of AAC, current available AAC models and devices, and AAC services (including assessment and intervention).

CHARACTERISTICS OF LANGUAGE DEVELOPMENT

Communication and Gestures

Many individuals with ASD did not develop spoken language in the typical way. This makes it difficult to evaluate their language development based solely on the spoken language component. Since gestures, speech, and language are tightly coupled neurologically and developmentally, researchers believe that gesture provides another means to examine underlying cognitive processes when expressive language is impaired (McNeill, 1992). In other words, it is critical to look at both speech and gestures when evaluating language development of children with ASD.

For typically developing children, rhythmic hand movements (e.g., banging objects) and vocalizations (e.g., babbling) emerge at approximately the same time (Capone & McGregor, 2004). For example, a 10-month-old baby—who can comprehend 10 words and demonstrates variegated bubbles—is able to make deictic gestures, such as showing, giving, and pointing. Along with the development of language and speech, a baby's hand gestural movement becomes more and more refined.

AUTISM AND GESTURE

Children with ASD demonstrate deviance in both language and gesture development (Capone & McGregor, 2004). Preverbal children with ASD communicate less frequently and use less complex combinations of gestures (Capone & McGregor, 2004). Also, atypical gestures or the lack of certain gestures (e.g., declarative gestures) are often observed among children with ASD (Camaioni, Perucchini, Muratori, Parrini, & Cesari, 2003). For example, Mundy & Burnette (2005) found that proto-declarative gestures (e.g., using index fingers to show something with a social intent) are less likely to be seen, whereas proto-imperative gestures (e.g., using fingers to indicate wanting something) are functional among children with ASD.

 Did you know:

• Children with ASD use other people's hands as tools.
• Children with ASD have difficulty with imitation skills.

- Diversity of object play could be one of the prognostic predictors for children with autism (Yoder, 2006).
- Children with ASD who explore objects in an atypical way at 12 months are likely to be lower functioning at later ages (Ozonoff et al., 2008).

ASD AND PRAGMATIC COMMUNICATION DISORDER

According to the *Diagnostic and Statistical Manual of Mental Disorders* (DSM-5), the newest diagnostic manual, pragmatic (or social) communication disorder is one of the major characteristics of children with ASD (American Psychiatric Association, 2013a, 2013b). Pragmatic communication disorder refers to the impaired use of communication in social contexts, including social communication and social interaction. However, many individuals with ASD exhibit more than just pragmatic communication deficits (e.g., absence of eye contact, failure to initiate or maintain social interaction).

ASD AND OTHER COMMUNICATION DISORDERS

In addition to social communication disorders, some people with ASD might have difficulties with aspects of verbal speech and language, such as articulation and semantics. Among these children, about 15 to 25 percent have been identified as nonverbal or people with complex communication needs. People with complex communication needs are those who cannot communicate their needs via conventional means, that is, speech. Thus, for this group of individuals, a different means of communication can be introduced to replace or augment speech, which is called augmentative and alternative communication (AAC). More about AAC will be discussed below.

Two common communication disorders found in those with ASD are:

Echolalia: The repetition of sounds, words, or sentences spoken by their communication partners. It can be delayed or immediate.

Hyperlexia: Some individuals with ASD are hyperlexic, which means that they possess word-decoding skills and have a relatively intact phonetic structure of words, but are impaired in abstract reasoning and reading comprehension.

Communication Disorder Simulation

Ask students to simulate a communication disorder associated with autism or other severe disabilities for 1–2 hours. During the simulation, each student must interact with at least two strangers.

- Date:
- Time:
- Location:
- Task:

- Describe the type of communication disorders you simulated:
- Describe how you simulated the disability:
- Describe what you did during the time (e.g., tasks):
- Describe the surrounding (e.g., how many people around):
- Describe difficulties you encountered:
- Describe other's reaction:
- Your personal thoughts regarding this experience:

WHAT IS AAC?

AAC stands for augmentative and alternative communication. The American Speech and Hearing Association (ASHA) defines AAC as follows:

> Augmentative and alternative communication (AAC) includes all forms of communication (other than oral speech) that are used to express thoughts, needs, wants, and ideas.

Although the term sounds foreign, we all use forms of AAC to communicate with others through facial expression, gestures, pictures, and symbols (ASHA, nd).

WHO NEEDS AAC?

Besides the individual with ASD mentioned earlier, some people with severe disability (SD) need AAC to communicate their wants and needs. "Severe disability" is an inclusive term that includes those who require "extensive and pervasive support" throughout life (Luckasson et al., 1992; Browder, Spooner & Meier, 2011). These individuals may have severe or profound intellectual disabilities, severe physical disabilities (e.g., cerebral palsy), or sensory disabilities (e.g., blind or deaf), or multiple disabilities. For the purposes of this chapter, individuals with SD are referred to as individuals with limited functional speech who require AAC. AAC can augment residual speech or provide alternative means during communication. People may have a temporary or permanent need for AAC, and may have some speech (augmentative communication) or no speech (alternative communication).

Question: Greg, a 10-year-old boy, has cerebral palsy (CP) and is able to communicate verbally with his parents at home using his residual speech. Does he need AAC?

Answer: Although Greg is able to communicate with familiar communication partners (e.g., his parents), unfamiliar communication partners (e.g., people at a grocery store) find his speech difficult to understand. Therefore, it is recommended that Greg also use AAC to supplement his natural speech. It is important for parents and teachers to think and act early. Imagine a few years later, Greg wants to make a public speech and has no reliable and familiar AAC system in place for him.

MYTHS/FACTS ABOUT AAC

AAC is distinct from assistive technology (AT): Many people mistakenly think AAC is part of AT, or even the same thing as AT. While there is some overlap between the two, AAC refers to an activity or process related to communication, including unaided communication (which does not require physical artifacts) and aided communication (which requires a physical tool, as does AT). On the other hand, AT is a tool or artifact used to assist people in performing tasks (communication, academia, leisure, etc.). AT also refers to a service related to selection, evaluation, and use of an AT device.

UNAIDED AND AIDED AAC

Unaided AAC

There are two types of AAC: unaided and aided. Unaided AAC refers to AAC that does not require any artifacts, such as manual signs, gestures, and fingerspelling. Unaided systems work well during children-directed activities. However, there are some disadvantages of unaided AAC, related to the training. Just as speech-language pathologists (SLP) need to know a great deal of sign language, the children's communication partners need to be educated as well.

Carson is a four-year-old child with ASD. He is a very active boy who likes to throw everything within reach. Carson has been practicing using picture symbols to communicate, but it has been hard for him to focus on pictures; he ends up tossing the pictures on the floor. An SLP then introduced manual signs during Carson's floor time. The SLP found that this unaided system worked really well because it eliminated time to make or find the target pictures.

When there was a teachable moment, the SLP could sign words to Carson and use hand-over-hand techniques to teach him. For example, once when Carson was thirsty, the SLP taught him how to sign, "water." A few weeks later Carson's mom told the SLP that Carson had come to her at night and asked for a drink by using the sign for "water."

Aided AAC

The second category is aided AAC, which is a big component in AAC. Unlike unaided AAC, which is produced by using the body to communicate, aided AAC requires tangible artifacts. We will discuss it from three aspects: devices (i.e., tangible artifacts), symbols (e.g., conveying messages), and access modes.

Devices

AAC ranges from low-tech (i.e., lite-tech) to high-tech AAC, depending on the complexity of the artifact or device. Although the discussion is unclear on what devices are considered low-, mid-, or high-tech, typically low- or lite-tech AAC refers to those nonelectronic, inexpensive devices that require little training to use. Teachers, family members, or therapists can usually make low- or lite-tech AAC devices.

On the other side of the spectrum, high-tech AAC devices are those made with electronic circuitry or computers. They are generally high in cost and require training to learn how to operate them. Users can rarely create this class of devices without a background in electrical circuitry, mechanics, or computer programming.

Symbols

You can find different types of symbols to present messages on AAC devices, such as pictures, line drawing, letters, and words. We can roughly characterize symbols into two groups: symbol systems and symbol sets. The main difference between symbol systems and symbol sets is the level of rules and logic behind them.

Symbol systems.   In general, symbol systems are governed by generative rules or logic to expend their symbols. In other words, you cannot create your own symbols. Common examples of symbol systems are written languages, such as English words or Chinese characters. Another less familiar example of a symbol system is Blissymbols. Blissymbols is a graphical language that uses bliss characters to form over 3,000 symbols. For example, an "animal" character plus a "feeling" character will form "pet." Blissymbols is more popular in Europe; however, the number of people using this symbol system is still unknown. Here is a website to show you how to combine different bliss-characters to form different meanings: http://www.iicm.tugraz.at/thesis/ahollosi_html/node9.html.

Symbol sets.   Compared to symbol systems, symbol sets are more widely used in the field of AAC. One reason is that with a symbol set it is easier to expand messages because there are no rules or logic behind the expansion of symbols. Everyone, including teachers and parents, can create his/her own symbol sets. They might include a real object, pictures, or drawings to represent different meanings or concepts.

Currently, there are quite a few commercially available symbol sets on the market, such as Picture Communication Symbols (PCS), Picsyms, and Minspeak. Some of these symbol sets are used on an AAC device, and some of the symbols may be created using their own software program, which can be purchased by teachers or parents.

When selecting symbol systems or symbol sets, we need to consider its concreteness (ease of recognition) and match it with an individual's cognitive abilities. Mirenda & Locke (1989) put different symbol types in an order based on the degree of iconicity. The order is, from the most iconic to the least iconic: objects, color photographs, black-and-white photographs, miniature objects, black-and-white line drawings, Blissymbols, and traditional orthography. Currently a new symbol set called True Object Based Icons (TOBI) uses an actual-size cut-out photo (see Taylor & Preece, 2010).

The hierarchy provides a general guideline when selecting appropriate symbols for an individual; however, it does not mean that everyone has the same view regarding iconicity. For example, some might view miniature objects as more concrete than color photos. Therefore, it is important to conduct a symbol assessment to determine the best symbol types.

Symbol Iconicity

Ask students to create the following symbols for an object of their choice (e.g., a cup) and rate each symbol's iconicity

- Object
- TOBI
- Color photograph
- Black-and-white photograph
- Miniature object
- Line drawing
- Blissymbol
- Traditional orthography

Access Modes

The third component of aided AAC is access methods, or how a person accesses messages on an AAC device. There are two major access modes: direct and indirect. Direct selection refers to a person directly "pointing" to target selection. By "pointing," a person can use one of the following to directly access the target messages: (a) use one's body parts (finger, toes) to physically touch the messages; (b) use an object (e.g., head stick) to touch the target messages; or (c) use eye gaze or an object (e.g., light pointer or a sensor) attached to a body part (usually one's head) to directly indicate the target messages without physically touching them. Direction selection is often (although not always) easier to learn and use, faster, and more accurate. People without physical limitations typically use their fingers to directly operate a device. Those with physical limitations can either use fingers coupled with a keyguard, which is attached on an AAC device, or other methods mentioned above.

People with physical limitations can also use the other access mode, indirect selection, often called "scanning." Indirection selection, or scanning, is a more passive access mode compared to direct selection. The person cannot directly select messages. It requires either manual scanning (operated by a communication partner when using a low-tech communication board) or automated scanning (operated by a machine when using a high-tech communication board).

When using manual scanning, the communication partner will point to messages one by one and the AAC user will signal his/her choice by nodding, vocalizing, or in some other reliable way. This method is usually employed using a low-tech AAC board, and with a familiar communication partner. On the other hand, when using automated scanning, the machine will scan the symbols using one of the scanning patterns (see below), and the AAC user will select the target using a switch or a blink.

Scanning patterns.   Before we talk about scanning modes, we need to know that there are different types of scanning patterns:

1. Scanning individual messages one by one in a linear way or in a circular way.
2. Row/column scanning: scanning each row first and then scanning each message across columns within the row. Column/row scanning is similar but begins with the columns and then the rows.

3. Scanning each group first and then scanning individual messages within the group.

Scanning modes. After determining the scanning pattern, we can then select a scanning mode. There are three different scanning modes available when using automated scanning. Choosing the best type is based on the AAC user's physical capability and sensory/cognitive alertness (Cook & Polgar, 2015). The choices are:

- Automatic: The scan of messages begins automatically and continually scans until the user presses the switch upon seeing the target message.
- Step: The user presses the switch to scan messages (which can be individual messages or a row/column of messages) one by one. Once the user hits the target messages/row/column, he/she can either select the target by stopping on it for a set amount of time, allowing the device to make the selection (when using a single switch), or by activating a second switch to make the selection (when using two switches).
- Inverse: The user begins scanning by pressing and holding the switch. The scanning will continue until the user reaches the target message and releases the switch, making the selection.

When helping a user to select the most appropriate way to activate switches, we need to make sure: (a) to consider direct selection first and use indirect as a backup; (b) if possible, to have at least two switches (one mover switch and one selector switch) to save time; and (c) if possible, to comb through direct selection and scanning to decrease fatigue.

INTERVENTION

Recognize Barriers

AAC barriers are things that hinder the effectiveness of an AAC intervention and a user's willingness to use an AAC device. It is critical to recognize the potential barriers related to the use of AAC so that therapists can address the barriers early on. Crisp et al. conducted an interview and found that barriers include: "poor voice quality, the unwieldiness of the devices, and the complexity involved in programming them" (Crisp et al., 2014: p. 232). Other barriers include: "lack of professional help (e.g., taking a long time to get a speech generating device [SGD]), negative reactions of others, and limited financial support." In addition, faulty understanding of communication style, common in autism (e.g., impaired social communication skills, hyperlexia), can be a barrier to AAC service. Some parents think that their children with autism understand their speech and thus believe the AAC service is not necessary (Hines, Balandin & Togher, 2011).

Recognizing Facilitators

It is also important to recognize facilitators that aid AAC intervention. Crisp, Draucker, and Ellett (2014) identified facilitators associated with the successful use of AAC and the increased use of AAC devices: appropriate voice, versatility of the device (e.g., allowing children to access the Internet or connect to other accessories), access to the AAC device outside of school, early intervention, allowing users to test-drive the devices in the evaluation process, and the user's ability to engage with peers and use developmentally appropriate language. It is interesting to note that parents prefer lightweight, portable, and versatile devices, such as the iPhone and iPad.

Cultural Competence

When providing AAC service, we need to consider not only the AAC users but also the AAC user's communication circles, including family, school, and community (Vanbiervliet & Parette, 2002). A competent cultural and linguistic therapist will consider various cultural factors such as ethnicity, sexual orientation, and social economic status, then modify the intervention accordingly. In addition, a therapist needs to be able to provide a supportive environment in which to facilitate participation of the family members during the planning and implementation phase (Vanbiervliet & Parette, 2002).

For example, 10-year-old Naim, with complex communication needs, is from a bilingual family where his grandparents and parents speak Arabic and his siblings predominantly speak English at home. Therefore, when working with Naim and his family during AAC assessment and interventions, the therapist and teacher need to make sure to incorporate two language systems in his AAC device. In addition, the therapist must make sure the vocabulary in his AAC device includes items that match their daily lifestyle.

INTERVENTION STRATEGIES

Color Arrangement on the Display

Because AAC access relies heavily on visual processing, teachers and parents need to pay attention to the display and the arrangement of icons on both low-tech and high-tech devices. Appropriate layout and arrangement of icons on an AAC board can decrease AAC users' cognitive loads, increase speed, and facilitate communication.

Among the factors that affect the visual process of an AAC board, color cueing and spatial arrangement of icons have the highest clinical values and the most supporting evidence from research (e.g., Wilkinson, O'Neill & McIlvane, 2014). For example, Wilkinson et al. used eye-tracking technology to confirm that AAC displays use like-colored icons arranged in a cluster manner to facilitate speed as compared to like-colored icons arranged in a distributed manner. In addition, an arrangement using like-colored icons clustered together on an AAC display can decrease the likelihood of distraction for students with autism, who tend to fixate on irrelevant details.

Low-Tech Communication Board

Ask students to complete a communication profile for an individual with complex communication needs. Based on the profile, each student will create a low-tech communication board.

For the profile:

- Please include the following information: Age, gender, cultural background, interests/personality, communication style, and relevant information about vision/hearing/mobility cognition/language skills.

For AAC board:

- It should have a minimum of 20 symbols (maximum 32) on the board.
- Although not required, students can use Boardmaker Online to create a communication (AAC) board.

How to access Boardmaker Online:

First, register as a new user on the website;
    https://www.boardmakeronline.com/lo-
  gin.aspx?ReturnUrl=/You/Home

Then, go to "Get Started," and select "Create Activities." The website will take you to their Internet app where you may create your own communication board on line.

Speed vs. Relevance

Let's try to say a sentence using a speed of four seconds per word: My----name----is----Karen----it----is----nice----to----meet----you. It is frustrating, isn't it? This is the speed with which a typical AAC user produces sentences using either letter-based or word-based systems on an AAC device. Speed is always a concern for AAC users. Therefore, some AAC devices provide what is called an "utterance-based system" that allows AAC users to select pre-stored complete phrases to use in communication. Even though communication speed is an important factor for effective communication, speed cannot be a trade-off when it comes to relevance of conversation.

Utterance-based systems use one of three strategies when encountering a situation in which the stored messages are not suitable for the conversation: (a) use of a pre-stored message without further editing; (b) revision of the pre-stored message on the fly; or (c) use of a conversational "floorholder" (e.g., "please wait, I am typing a message") to inform the listener to please wait while the user edits a pre-stored message. Despite the faster delivery when using the pre-stored messages without editing, it is actually the least favored strategy according to AAC users' communication partners (Bedrosian, Hoag, & McCoy, 2003). A communication partner's preference is usually in favor of a slow but relevant conversation with a "floorholder" than with a faster, but less relevant conversation (Bedrosian et al., 2003).

Comparing Speech Generating Devices (SGDs)

There are two major companies (Dynavox, and Prentke Romich Company [PRC]) that make SGD devices. The frameworks behind these two companies are quite different; each has its own advantages and disadvantages. PRC is using a semantics-based procedure in which they adopt the Unity language system. This system has a consistent set of icons and arrangement, which can enhance automatic motor movement (i.e., motor planning) to save time searching for icons during conversations (Halloran, 2004). The Unity system focuses on core vocabulary use (i.e., the 300–400 most commonly used words, which comprise 70–80 percent of speech; Marvin, Beukelman & Bilyeu, 1994). Each unity icon has multiple meanings depending on how the subsequent icons are combined. For example, the picture of an apple can represent a single message or an apple, or it can mean "eat" if combined with the adjective icon for "hungry." Individuals in favor of the Unity system like the consistent arrangement of the icons and how it mimics the grammatical system and language development. However, this system requires more intensive training, not only for users but also therapists, family members, etc.

Dynavox is adopting a theme-based organization (including icons of some core words, a folder containing food items, and a folder containing toys). Therefore, a person can find the word "apple" in the food folder and the word "hungry" in the describing folder.

Dynavox also provides another display called visual scene display. The visual scene display uses a background picture, such as a room and context related to the scene (e.g., choices of toys, objects in the room), to provide contextual support (Blackstone, 2005; Wilkinson, Light, & Drager, 2012). Teachers can import pictures or use pre-stored background pictures to modify or add to a relevant vocabulary folder, or add areas or hot spots to make the scene interactive.

HOW TO INCORPORATE AAC AT HOME, SCHOOL, AND IN THE COMMUNITY

Here is another exercise to aid students in understanding and using AAC. Divide the students into groups of three members and discuss appropriate interventions or strategies for each of the following scenarios:

Scenario 1

Jacob is a four-year-old boy with autism who is nonverbal and has been able to use at least basic signs independently to request objects/activities and to greet people, including signs for "more," "water," "cookies," "hi," "music," "play," and "car." However, the therapist noticed that Jacob does not use these signs with his parents and older brother at home. What can the therapist do to help the parents and the brother better communicate with Jacob, and to ensure that Jacob will be able to utilize what he learns in the clinic in his home environment as well?

Hints: The therapist can provide training to the parents on how to sign, when to sign, and how to provide feedback and correction to Jacob. The therapist can also teach the parents how to train the brother to do the same. Furthermore, the therapist can use worksheets to make sure the family practices these signs at home and in the community.

Scenario 2

Jessica is a fifth-grade student with cerebral palsy. She attends a public school and is enrolled in a general education classroom. She uses an SGD device in school to communicate with her peers, 50 percent of the time. She uses residual speech at home to communicate with her mom. However, as noticed by her teacher, Mr. Jackson, Jessica barely uses her Vintage, an SGD device, in the classroom to participate in class discussions or to raise questions. Her teacher wants to know how to help Jessica to be more involved in the science class.

Hints: Mr. Jackson will pre-store questions in Jessica's AAC device. When Jessica takes time to type out her messages, Mr. Jackson will model for his students how to converse with an AAC user by waiting patiently and reacting normally, as he would to other students.

Scenario 3

Marc is a 25-year-old male with autism. Every Saturday he likes to go to a local restaurant to dine with his family. He likes to order the same dish and has a pre-stored message in his AAC device. One day in the restaurant, the waiter told Marc that his favorite dish had been sold out and asked if he would like to order something else. How should Marc and his parents react?

Hints: Individuals with ASD sometimes do not react well to changes in their routine. Therefore, parents can remind Marc to use what is called a "floorholder," such as "Please wait. I need some time to type my message." In this case it is used as a strategy to repair a possible communication breakdown, giving Marc time to formulate his message.

PICTURE EXCHANGE COMMUNICATION SYSTEM

Picture Exchange Communication System (PECS) is an AAC intervention package initially designed in 1985 for individuals with ASD, and is now also used with other individuals with severe disabilities (PECS, n.d.). PECS requires extensive training for individuals to carry out the intervention during each phase, as well as for those who receive the interventions. The initial goal of PECS is to have a user request the desired object by exchange of a symbol, and then progress to a phase where they can format their request using a string of icons. There are multiple steps involved in PECS. Students are required to master each step before moving on to the next. Mastery is considered to be a score of 85 percent accuracy out of 10 given opportunities. The following is a very general overview of each of the six phases (Frost & Bondy, 2000).

Phase 1. Physically Assisted Exchange: An individual gives a picture symbol to a communicative partner to gain access to a desired item. The goal is to teach students the sequence of picture exchange: pick up (the picture of a desired item), reach (toward the communicative partner), and release (the picture into the trainer's hand), at which point the child will be rewarded with the desired item. Two trainers are needed: one communicative partner, who sits across from the child, and one physical prompter, who sits behind the child to physically guide the child's picture exchange behavior.

Phase 2. Expanding Spontaneity: In this phase, the child goes to his/her communication book, pulls out a picture of a desired item, walks toward his/her communicative partner, and releases the picture into the partner's hand. Use only one picture (placing the target picture outside of the binder). The distance between the student and the communicative partner is gradually increased, as is the distance between the student and the communication book. The physical prompting will help the student move toward the communicative partner and the book.

Phase 3. Simultaneous Discrimination of Pictures: The goal is for the child to be able to request desired items by choosing the correct picture when shown pictures of a desired item and a non-preferred item or neutral object. Using systematic ways to help the child discriminate inappropriate pictures from the picture of a desired item, start with a foil picture, then a faded picture of a non-preferred item, and then a regular picture of the non-preferred item.

Phase 4. Sentence Structure: The goal is to help students place a sequence of pictures on a sentence strip (e.g., an "I want" picture and a reinforcing picture) to build a sentence structure requesting the desired item.

Phase 5. Responding to "What do you want?": The goal is for the student to answer the question "What do you want?" by placing a sequence of pictures on a sentence strip ("I want" and a reinforcing picture) and handing the strip to the communicative partner.

Phase 6. Responsive and spontaneous commenting: The goal is for the child to be able to make a comment by placing a sequence of pictures on a sentence strip. Tangible or social rewards are then used to reinforce the child's correct choices.

Please note that the above information is a very basic introduction of PECS. If you are considering using PECS with your children or students in the future, you will need to contact a professional and undergo formal training on PECS.

PECS Devices

There are low-tech to high-tech selections of PECS devices. A low-tech PECS is a binder consisting of symbols and a sentence strip with Velcro. The sentence strip can be removed from the binder and handed to a communication partner. An example of mid-tech PECS is the LOGAN ProxTalker. It uses radio frequency identification technology to prerecord sound onto tags (i.e., electronic chips) and play them back when the user places one on any of the buttons on the device. Since it can play the prerecorded sounds, it can also be considered as an SGD (Boesch, Wendt, Subramanian & Hsu, 2013). The price for a single unit is around $2,495. The company offers a four-week trial for $75. Currently, PECS can be administered using a portable tablet, such as an iPad, that is equipped with a PECS app.

Scenario: Dave is a five-year-old boy with ASD who has limited speech. His favorite playthings are toy cars. Describe the materials; trainers; and (teaching) strategies (e.g., verbal prompting) you might need for teaching each phase.

Phase	Materials Needed	Trainer(s)/Personnel's needed	Prompting needed
Phase 1			
Phase 2			
Phase 3			
Phase 4			
Phase 5			
Phase 6			

Figure 5.1.   Activity: Using the 6 phases, create a plan for PECS use.
Source: Pei-Lin Weng

CURRENT ISSUES AND TRENDS

AAC has undergone a major revolution in terms of users and family gaining access, thanks to the accessibility of mobile devices equipped with AAC apps. In the past, because of the high cost of an AAC device (particularly an SGD, which can cost into the thousands), the process of obtaining an AAC device required extensive work including assessment, feature matching, funding application, and approval. The whole process could take as long as a year before the student could have access.

Now, parents could spend a few hundred dollars for an iPad, buy an AAC app for about $200, and gain immediate access to an AAC device for their children. Although it seems like an easy way out, caution is advised. Parents, teachers, and professionals should scrutinize the accessibility of such AAC devices for individuals to be sure the choice is not based only on the familiarity of a particular technology (Light & McNaughton, 2013).

SUMMARY

Individuals with ASD/SD do not develop linguistic capabilities in the same manner as typically developing children. Babies with autism may develop fewer meaningful gestures, and later may be very slow to develop verbal skills. Pragmatics become difficult as these children lack understanding of social contexts, like making eye contact. Language deficits may consist of echolalia and hyperlexia, along with an inability to initiate conversation or sustain discussion.

AAC refers to the means that may be used by individuals with ASD/SD to help them communicate. These fall into two categories: assisted and unassisted communications. Unassisted communication is accomplished several ways, such as the use of ASL, or American Sign Language. Assisted Technology, or AT, refers to the use of some sort of tool or technology to enable the individual with ASD/SD to communicate thoughts more clearly.

AT devices range from low-tech (such as Blissymbols) to high-tech (like PECS) and could, in some cases, run into many thousands of dollars to obtain. However, with the advent of smartphones and tablets, many AAC applications have been developed that may be purchased at modest prices, to bring some of the newest developments in AT within the reach of much of today's society.

REFERENCES

American Psychiatric Association. (2013a). Autism spectrum disorder fact sheet. Retrieved from http://www.dsm5.org/Documents/Autism%20Spectrum%20Disorder%20Fact%20Sheet.pdf.

American Psychiatric Association. (2013b). *Diagnostic and statistical manual of mental disorders*, 5th ed. Arlington, VA: American Psychiatric Publishing.

Bedrosian, J. L., Hoag, L. A., & McCoy, K. F. (2003). Relevance and speed of message delivery trade-offs in augmentative and alternative communication. *Journal of Speech, Language, and Hearing Research, 46*(4), 800–17.

Blackstone, S. (2005). What are visual scene displays. *RERC on Communication Enhancement, 1*(2).

Boesch, M. C., Wendt, O., Subramanian, A., & Hsu, N. (2013). Comparative efficacy of the Picture Exchange Communication System (PECS) versus a speech-generating device: Effects on requesting skills. *Research in Autism Spectrum Disorders, 7*(3), 480–93.

Browder, D. M., Spooner, F., & Meier, I. (2011). Introduction. In D. M. Browder & F. H. Spooner (Eds.), *Teaching students with moderate and severe disabilities* (pp. 3–11). New York: Guilford Press.

Camaioni, L., Perucchini, P., Muratori, F., Parrini, B., & Cesari, A. (2003). The communicative use of pointing in autism: developmental profile and factors related to change. *European Psychiatry, 18*(1), 6–12.

Capone, N. C., & McGregor, K. K. (2004). Gesture development: A review for clinical and research practices. *Journal of Speech, Language, and Hearing Research, 47*(1), 173–86.

Cook, A. M., & Polgar , J. M. (2015). *Assistive technologies: Principles and practice*, 4th. ed. St. Louis, MO: Mosby/Elsevier.

Crisp, C., Draucker, C. B., & Ellett, M. L. C. (2014). Barriers and facilitators to children's use of speech-generating devices: a descriptive qualitative study of mothers' perspectives. *Journal for Specialists in Pediatric Nursing, 19*(3), 229–37.

Frost, L., & Bondy, A. (2000). An Introduction to PECS [DVD]. Pyramid Educational Consultants UK.

Halloran, J. (2004). Minspeak and Unity. Retrieved from:https://www.prentrom.com/training_materials/MinspeakandUnity.pdf.

Hines, M., Balandin, S., & Togher, L. (2011). Communication and AAC in the lives of adults with autism: The stories of their older parents. *Augmentative and Alternative Communication, 27*(4), 256–66.

Light, J., & McNaughton, D. (2013). Putting people first: Re-thinking the role of technology in augmentative and alternative communication intervention. *Augmentative and Alternative Communication, 29*(4), 299–309.

Luckasson, R., Coulter, D., Polloway, E. A., Reiss, S., Schalock, R. L., Snell, M. E., et al. (1992). *Mental retardation: Definition, classification, and systems of supports.* Washington, DC: AAMR.

Marvin, C., Beukelman, D., & Bilyeu, D. (1994). Vocabulary-use patterns in preschool children: Effects of context and time sampling. *Augmentative & Alternative Communication, 10*: 224–36.

McNeill, D. (1992). *Hand and mind: What gestures reveal about thought.* Chicago: University of Chicago Press.

Mirenda, P., & Locke, P. A. (1989). A comparison of symbol transparency in nonspeaking persons with intellectual disabilities. *Journal of Speech and Hearing Disorders, 54*(2), 131–40.

Mundy, P., & Burnette, C. (2005). Joint attention and neurodevelopment. In F.R. Volkmar, R. Paul, A. Klin, & D. Cohen (Eds.), *Handbook of autism and pervasive developmental disorders.* Volume I: *Diagnosis, development, neurobiology, and behavior,* 3rd ed. (pp. 650–81). Hoboken, NJ: Wiley.

Ozonoff, S., Macari, S., Young, G. S., Goldring, S., Thompson, M., & Rogers, S. J. (2008). Atypical object exploration at 12 months of age is associated with autism in a prospective sample. *Autism, 12*(5), 457–72.

PECS. (n.d.). What is PECS? Retrieved from http://www.pecsusa.com/pecs.php.

Taylor, K., & Preece, D. (2010). Using aspects of the TEACCH structured teaching approach with students with multiple disabilities and visual impairment: Reflections on practice. *British Journal of Visual Impairment, 28*(3), 244–59.

Vanbiervliet, A., & Parette, H. P. (2002). Development and evaluation of the Families, Cultures and Augmentative and Alternative Communication (AAC) multimedia program. *Disability & Rehabilitation, 24*(1–3), 131–43.

Wilkinson, K. M., O'Neill, T., & McIlvane, W. J. (2014). Eye-tracking measures reveal how changes in the design of aided AAC displays influence the efficiency of locating symbols by school-age children without disabilities. *Journal of Speech, Language, and Hearing Research, 57*(2), 455–66.

Wilkinson, K. M., Light, J., & Drager, K. (2012). Considerations for the composition of visual scene displays: Potential contributions of information from visual and cognitive sciences. *Augmentative and Alternative Communication, 28*(3), 137–47.

Yoder, P. J. (2006). Predicting lexical density growth rate in young children with autism spectrum disorders. *American Journal of Speech-Language Pathology, 15*(4), 378–88.

Chapter Six

Facilitating Inclusive Opportunities in School and Community

Peter Griswold

Ms. Celeste Everyteacher is facing her elementary education class on a pleasant Indian summer morning in early September. She is pleased with the language arts lesson she has created and is looking forward to teaching it to a semi-eager group of fifth graders. She has aligned her learning outcomes and instruction to a Common Core Standard: "Write opinion pieces on topics or texts, supporting a point of view with reasons and information" (CCSS.ELA-Literacy.W.5.1). Students will accomplish the learning objective by writing a letter either for or against a plan to construct a water park next to a state forest.

Ms. E. plans to introduce the lesson by having students imagine they are taking a walk in cool, dark woodlands. She will describe the sounds, sights, and smells they might encounter, and ask them to add their own impressions. She will introduce the vocabulary the students will need to understand and use in their letter (e.g., *commission, wildlife, leisure, rural, environment*) and then provide a context for the speech: A company has applied to an Environmental Protection Commission to construct a water park next to the state forest. The students' task is to write a letter expressing their opinion as to whether the Commission should give permission, and provide support for their opinion.

For practice, Ms. E. will give the students a worksheet with the vocabulary words and matching meanings, and together, the class will write an opinion essay on whether children should have to eat healthy foods even if they don't like them. The students will then work in small groups to brainstorm ideas for their letter. One student will take notes, which will be distributed to the rest of the group, and the students will write a first draft on their own.

Beaming with pleasure, Ms. E. commenced the lesson. Before describing how the lesson progressed, let's analyze two elements of teaching, elements that perhaps Ms. E. has not overtly acknowledged, but which guide and inform her planning and teaching. The first element is: What are her expectations? Through various sources, perhaps past experience; education courses; the district curriculum; the teacher's edition of a language arts text; or the advice of mentors, Ms. E. has developed certain expectations of what the students in her fifth-grade class should be able to accomplish. Those expectations form the basis for her instruction; in this case, the expectation is that the students will be able to produce a letter that meets the learning objective.

The second is a related element, the predictability of events in the classroom. Ms. E. believes that the lesson will unfold as she has envisioned it, with students describing what they see and hear in the forest, paying attention as she presents the vocabulary words, completing the vocabulary worksheet correctly, contributing to the practice opinion piece, participating in the group discussion, and writing a letter expressing an opinion and supporting it with logical reasons.

For most of the children in the classroom, the lesson worked well and the learning objective was met. However, Ms. E. felt upset and frustrated when she finished the lesson because one child (we'll call him Trevor) was not able to participate appropriately and produce a grade-level letter. Trevor has been classified with autism spectrum disorder (ASD), and experienced difficulty at nearly every point in the lesson. During the introduction, he was confused when asked to imagine taking a walk through the forest. During the teaching, he didn't understand what was involved in expressing an opinion and supporting it with reasons and information. He also had difficulty understanding the role of the Environmental Protection Commission.

Trevor did well with the matching exercise on the vocabulary worksheet, but began to argue with other students who expressed different opinions about whether or not children should eat healthy foods even if they don't like them. He didn't participate in the small group discussions and couldn't recall the format of a letter, explain the reasons for his opinion, or use any of the vocabulary terms in his writing. In short, Ms. E's expectations were frustrated, and the lesson took several unpredictable turns.

Ms. E's first thought was to question whether Trevor belonged in her class. She wondered if his needs for instruction, at his functioning level, could better be met in a special education classroom with a teacher trained to teach children with ASD. The answer was that Trevor did belong in Ms. E's class simply because that is where his individual education plan (IEP) stated that he would be placed. The IEP team, composed of Trevor's parents, a general education teacher, a special education teacher, and his case manager, followed the guideline in federal law that states that:

> To the maximum extent appropriate, children with disabilities, including children in public or private institutions or other care facilities, are educated with children who are not disabled, and special classes, separate schooling, or other removal of children with disabilities from the regular educational environment occurs only when the nature or severity of the disability of a child is such that education in regular classes with the use of supplementary aids and services cannot be achieved satisfactorily. (IDEA 2004, Title 1/Part B/Section 612 (a)(5))

The members considered a number of factors in making a place-ment decision, including Trevor's strong motivation, and the mod-eling of behavior and social opportunities afforded by placement with nondisabled peers. The IEP team felt that the ultimate goal of preparing Trevor to live and work in the community would best be served by the general education setting. With adaptations, Trevor would be able to benefit from instruction in the general education classroom.

Although Trevor's IEP team was aware that he was not on grade level in language arts and had difficulty with whole and small group instruction, they felt that the gap was not so large as to prevent Trevor from learning from the teacher's instruction. They felt that, with strategies and modifications, he would be able to achieve his academic goals to the maximum extent possible. Those strategies were listed in Trevor's IEP.

As Ms. E. read about Trevor's needs in his IEP and thought about how the suggestions in the IEP could be applied to a specific lesson, she identified several strategies that would have helped Tre-vor. She realized that including a picture of a forest in the introduc-tion would have made it easier for Trevor to imagine what a walk in the forest was like. Perhaps she could even have identified a specif-ic park or forest with which the other children and Trevor were familiar.

For the vocabulary instruction, Ms. E. will go beyond the dic-tionary definition by providing visual aids, context, synonyms, an-tonyms, and associations with ideas that Trevor and the other stu-dents should recognize. Ms. E. will provide a model of a letter, then ask Trevor to name a food that he likes and tell whether he thinks it is healthy. She will appoint a leader in each small group whose task it is to make sure everyone has a chance to express an opinion, and she will give Trevor a graphic organizer to help him organize his ideas around an opinion and supporting detail. The IEP has helped Ms. E. adjust her expectations for Trevor and implement strategies that will make Trevor's responses to the lesson more predictable and productive.

A teacher's expectations and the predictability of events during a lesson are a way to begin a more general discussion about including students with ASD in the general education classroom. Children with ASD compel us to revise our expectations, individualizing them so that they represent what the child can reasonably accomplish.

We need to view students with ASD not in terms of the gap between the child's functioning level and grade-level standards, but in more productive ways, such as taking into consideration what the child has mastered up to this point, and what the next step in the curriculum is. The most destructive way to view a child with ASD (or any disability, for that matter) is to dismiss them as incapable of learning just because they are not near grade level. Instead, in areas of weakness, we should set individual goals high in order to challenge the student, but not so high as to eliminate any hope of attaining them.

Aids and supports are important because they greatly expand the inclusion of students with ASD into the general education classroom. Inclusion represents a change from years ago when students with disabilities were mainstreamed in areas where they were functioning on grade level. Given the benefits of and legal provision for inclusion, students with ASD are placed in the general education classroom with support where needed, but not beyond that need.

Inclusion can take several forms. Full inclusion occurs when a child is on the class roster and in the general education classroom, except when being "pulled out" for educational support or therapy. Partial inclusion occurs when a student is on the roster of a special education self-contained class and goes into the general education classroom at certain times, usually for specific subjects and/or activities. The premise is that the student with ASD will receive whatever supports and services are needed to make his or her inclusion in the general education classroom successful.

A primary example of support is the presence of a co-teacher, typically one trained in special education services. Other types of support include the provision of a classroom aide, the availability of consultations with experts in learning and behavior strategies, and the infusion of therapies (typically speech-language or occupational therapy) into the general education classroom.

Can teachers be helped to individualize expectations for children with ASD? The answer is complicated. The term "spectrum" means that, within the population of children with autism spectrum disorder, there will be a wide range of symptoms with varying degrees of severity. Because of this, there is no "typical" student with ASD in the general education classroom. The most prevalent characteristics of children with ASD include impairments with social communication and interaction, and "restricted, repetitive patterns of behavior, interests or activities" (Hardman, Drew & Egan, 2014: p. 272).

However, delays in communication can range all the way from children with severe ASD, who have no language, to those with echolalia, who repeat what has been said, to those whose language is marked by mild delays in grammar and expression or whose tone sounds unnaturally flat or formal. Similarly, some children with ASD exhibit repetitive movements that appear to be self-stimulatory, such as rocking and spinning. Others perseverate on a narrow topic of interest, such as train schedules. A third group may panic over small changes in routines or schedules, and a fourth group may be easily overwhelmed by loud noises or bright lights.

The IEP can help the teacher identify the characteristics of the individual child and the severity of their disability. In addition, the IEP will contain some generalized strategies and modifications for the student. The challenge for the teacher, whether special or general education, is how to apply those generalized adaptations to specific lessons. Past experience of teachers and aides who have worked with the child, and input from educational specialists is helpful, but the process of coming to know the child's capabilities vis-à-vis one's own teaching style and requirements is often one of trial and error.

Similarly, choosing the strategies and modifications that work with a specific child involves the willingness to gather a repertoire of adaptations and then experiment with different strategies to see which ones help. Reference books such as the *Pre-Referral Intervention Manual* by McCarney & Wunderlich (2014) are excellent resources. Other teachers, educational support staff, parents, and sometimes the children themselves may be sources of ideas.

The rest of this chapter describes strategies and adaptations that will help the child with ASD be as successful as possible in the general education classroom. The intent is not to introduce methods that require significant amounts of training and one-to-one time with a child during class time (for a discussion of intensive, specialized strategies for children with ASD, see Ryan, Hughes, Katsiyannis, McDaniel & Sprinkle, 2011). The strategies for the inclusion teacher must be within the capacity of a general education teacher or co-teacher without drawing him/her away from other students. Some may require advance preparation, while others can be implemented on the spot. The critical aspect is that they must not require significant amounts of class time to implement.

INITIAL CONSIDERATIONS IN PLANNING FOR THE CHILD WITH ASD IN THE INCLUSIVE CLASSROOM

Inclusion of children with ASD in the general education classroom serves a dual purpose. The first is a universal one: mastering academic skills. The second is the acquisition of functional skills. "Functional" refers to those skills needed for the daily routine in the settings in which one lives—the home, community, and the school (Hardman et al., 2014). At the preschool level, examples of functional skills include sharing toys, taking turns, and using the bathroom. At the elementary level, children need to keep track of their possessions, follow the rules and routines of the classroom, and find their way to the bathroom.

At the middle and high school level, as the demands for independence increase, examples include navigating around the school, purchasing items in the cafeteria, dressing for physical education classes, and using a locker. Important at all levels is the need to establish and maintain satisfactory personal interactions with peers and adults. When the child with ASD approaches adolescence, sex education and self-protection against bullies are additional areas that need to be addressed.

For higher-functioning children with ASD, the academic skills will have a priority along with social communication and interaction. For lower-functioning children with ASD, the functional skills that are needed in the classroom will assume greater importance. Barnhill (2011) provides examples of survival skills that are introduced in preschool and are needed for successful adjustment in K–12 grades: "complying with adult requests, taking turns, listening to directions from afar or near, sitting quietly during activities, volunteering, raising one's hand to solicit attention, walking in line . . . picking toys [and other possessions] up after use [and] communicating about basic needs" (p. 235).

One may ask: If functional skills are the priority, is the special education classroom the better place to teach them? Various researchers and other writers have advocated for inclusion for students with ASD but often with prerequisites for success.

In a study of young children with ASD and other disabilities, Kliewer et al. (2004) wrote that, "Inclusive education appeared to be fundamental to the literate citizenship of children with significant disabilities" (*Conclusions: Constructing Contexts of Support for Literacy*, paragraph 1). Biklen and Burke (2006) wrote that inclusive educators should presume competence of the child with ASD and search for ways to access that competence. Daily (2005) has posited that the general education setting, by offering more opportunities for social interaction, has more potential for enhancing social communication skills. Simon (2010) offered a balanced view of inclusion for children with ASD, commenting favorably on the presence of positive role models in the general education classroom, but also noting that the multitude of sights, sounds, and smells in a general education classroom can be frustrating, and the academic content too advanced or covered too quickly.

Both Daily and Simon were concerned about the lack of training for general education and co-teachers. Chandler-Olcott and Kluth (2009) wrote that the best place to teach literacy skills and strategies for life is in the general education classroom. Researchers argued that learning these skills in the wider community (in this case, the general education classroom) affords modeling by peers and better opportunities for generalization and maintenance (for a review of the literature, see White, Scahill, Klin, Koenig & Volkmar, 2007).

A second consideration is the ASD child's emotional state in the classroom. The tendency toward restricted and repetitive patterns of behavior, interests, and activities of children with ASD (Hardman et al., 2014) reflects the child's anxiety, an anxiety that the child attempts to mediate through adhering to inflexible behaviors and rigid routines. This helps give him or her a sense of control over what may seem an arbitrary and at times chaotic social and academic environment. For the child with ASD, the world is a confusing place.

Gill (2005) lists some aspects of the teaching/learning process that can produce anxiety in children with ASD: too many choices, open-ended tasks, vague directions, idioms, words with multiple meanings, sequencing, integrating and organizing information, trying to imagine something the student has never experienced, and identifying essential ideas. For these children, the ability to make sense of the general education classroom is compromised by difficulties in understanding the purposes of others' behaviors and the feelings behind them.

Maneuvering their way through the maze of classroom procedures and expectations is further complicated by impairments in communicating needs and relating to others. Thus, the child with ASD seeks predictability in his environment, and displays an over-reliance upon routine. Changes in schedules or classroom routines, and frustration with academic tasks, can result in the child with ASD becoming upset and sometimes acting out in the form of meltdowns or tantrums.

Strategies for addressing this include preparing the child for changes in the schedule such as warning the child that the teacher will be out of the room for a conference or that physical education is cancelled due to an assembly program. Talking with the children about the rationale for change in routine may help. Asking the child to verbalize his feelings is another option. For younger children, a strip with emoticons can help the child share his anxiety by identifying his/her feelings.

A third consideration is the type of language the teacher uses. Keeping in mind the impairments in receptive language of children with ASD, the teacher needs to express directions and explanations in as brief terms as possible. Qualifiers to directions should be stated in separate sentences. Simple, basic vocabulary should be used as much as possible to explain more abstract terms, and to check for understanding. "If . . . then . . ." sentences help children

Happy   Sad   Confused   Angry   Straight Face   Thinking   Worried   Not talking   Surprised

Figure 6.1.   Feelings Chart for the child with ASD. *Source: Peter Griswold*

with ASD understand consequences (e.g., "If you interrupt your friend's story, then he will feel upset.").

Similes, metaphors, and sarcasm are often difficult for children with ASD to understand and should be used with caution. Teasing and jokes can be misunderstood. A woman with autism wrote about a teacher who terrified her by telling her that she would have to stay in school overnight if she didn't finish an assignment by the end of the school day. As a child, the woman did not understand that the teacher was only joking (Hardman et al., 2014).

A fourth consideration is the reaction of other students in the class to the inclusion of a child with ASD. One aspect of the ASD child's presence in the room that might confuse or create conflict is the teacher's response to misbehavior. As part of a behavior intervention plan for the child with ASD, he or she may be praised or rewarded for good behavior that is not acknowledged with other children. For example, a target behavior of the child with ASD might be to remain in his/her seat during whole group lessons. If the child with ASD meets that standard they would be praised or earn some type of positive reinforcement. The teacher can minimize the situation by setting individual goals for other children, too, and praising the class for serving as good models.

Perhaps what the children will react to most are the unusual behaviors the child with ASD utilizes to cope with anxiety. For younger children who are learning proper behavior in the classroom, atypical behavior is confusing. For older children, unusual behavior may invite mockery, making the child with ASD a target for ridicule and isolation. Children's perceptions of their peers are a part of gaining independence in social relationships, and we must not underplay the challenges in the teacher's role and the sensitivity that is needed. When teasing or more serious behavior occurs, capable teachers can enforce the rule that students treat each other with respect in the classroom.

However, not every setting in the school is closely supervised, and children have ways to shame and reject each other that escape the notice of adults. While some teachers have had a discussion with the class about a child's disability before the child arrives, others have waited to gauge the reaction of the students and address specific situations. At times, teachers have held a discussion while the child is out of the classroom. It is important, however, to balance the confidentiality of the student against such a discussion of the child and his or her disorder.

Questions from other children reflect their curiosity, and sometimes their confusion. The teacher's judgment is needed in determining which questions to answer and how deep that answer should go. Older, higher-functioning children with ASD can sometimes speak for themselves or provide guidance for the teacher in how to explain their disability. The focus of the discussion should be on how the child with ASD can be helped to adjust. The teacher can point out that it is the job of the student with ASD to help everyone in the class feel comfortable, but he or she will need all the students' assistance to accomplish this.

The needs of the child with ASD can be placed in the context that at times everyone needs coaching to improve. The teacher can ask students to recall a time when they were struggling with a task and a teacher, coach, or family member offered a tip to help them succeed. This is an opportunity to draw the connection between the other children's experiences and times when the teacher reminds their classmate with ASD to squeeze a koosh ball when feeling anxious.

Promoting acceptance of the child with ASD is a crucial part of helping him or her feel secure in the general education classroom. It's important for the teacher to establish a positive classroom environment and model acceptance by using small gestures. Some examples might include taking the time to greet students as they come into the classroom, drawing them out to learn of their interests and activities, and expressing enthusiasm over their successes both inside and outside the classroom. Consider pairing the child with ASD with a peer assistant who can provide help with specific tasks, or establishing a peer-tutoring program in the classroom (for a more extended discussion on peer tutoring, see Mastropieri & Scruggs, 2014).

Plan an activity that promotes peer acceptance. For example, have the children sit in a circle. Give each child a turn sitting inside the circle. Then, going around the circle, every child must say one thing that they like about the child in the center. For older children, an equivalent activity would be to have each student write what they like about a designated child. The notes would be placed in a jar and presented to the designated child to read.

DIFFERENTIATING INSTRUCTION

Differentiating instruction is the process by which curriculum, instruction, practice, and assessment is individualized for children who differ in terms of readiness for instruction, learning style, and preferences. Differentiation can take fairly simple forms. The general education teacher or co-teacher may provide a model of the assignment, a template, or some additional one-to-one explanation and instruction after a whole group lesson. Extra time to complete an assignment, either in the classroom or by taking classroom assignments home, is a possibility. The number of math problems or items to be recalled on a test may be reduced. Students can be given a choice as to how they would like to demonstrate their learning.

Instead of a written test, students could write a song, create a math problem, or plan a journey. Assignments can be geared to student interests in areas such as popular culture, sports, or technology. This aspect needs to be handled carefully with some children with ASD, who may exhibit very intense interest in a quite narrow topic, such as maps. While the overall goal is to broaden the ASD child's range of topics, it is also possible to work the child's interest into assignments. For example, an ASD student with an interest in maps could complete math problems with distances on maps as a theme.

Additional strategies, some that require extra resources, are possibilities. Leveled texts, where the same ideas can be delivered at different reading levels, are available from publishers of educational materials (e.g., Shell Education). Scaffolding is a technique whereby the learner is helped to the final goal through a series of steps, for example, long-division problems with some of the numbers written in, questions on reading assignments with the page or paragraph number written in, or sentence starters and word banks for writing assignments. Sometimes just giving a student time to talk about a topic while a co-teacher or aide listens can fuel their processing of the information.

Tomlinson (1999) has written extensively on differentiating instruction at different levels, and has divided the learning process into three steps: content (what is taught and how it is taught); process (how the learner applies the key skills to understand essential ideas and information); and product (how the learner demonstrates the learning, and how it is assessed).

Differentiating begins with the curriculum. The teacher first decides whether the learning objectives are appropriate for the specific child with ASD. The next area to analyze is the style of instruction. Are the skills and information being presented in ways that engage the child's attention and enable him or her to process what is being seen and heard? The third area is guided and independent practice: Are the activities in which the child is actively applying skills and information suitable for developing mastery? Finally, will the child with ASD demonstrate mastery in the same way as the other children, or will a different method need to be implemented to more accurately assess the student's mastery?

Teachers need to look for opportunities for differentiation in any one of these four areas: curriculum, instruction, practice, and assessment. Differentiation of the curriculum is accomplished by the use of two processes: unpacking and tiering objectives. Tiering refers to the use of multiple levels of objectives.

One way to think about unpacking and tiering objectives is to analyze them in terms of cognitive skills. What is the student being asked to do? Are they to recall information, understand information, apply skills, analyze the parts of information (the traditional compare-and-contrast activity), synthesize something new, or evaluate information? Recalling and understanding are generally considered lower-level skills, and tiering objectives for children with ASD may involve a greater dependence upon these levels, with higher levels introduced judiciously according to the student's progress.

In unpacking the standards, we analyze the different levels of cognition that are required. Table 6.1 illustrates five components of cognition that are required for students to meet the Common Core State Standard in reading informational texts at the fifth-grade level.

Unpacking allows us to go to the next step of deciding how to tier the learning objective. Table 6.1 also contains an example of how a lower level of a common core standard allows the teacher to more accurately identify the level of understanding and analysis for a child with ASD in second grade (Dynamic Learning Maps, 2015).

In differentiating instruction, typically the visual modality is a stronger channel for learning than the auditory modality for children with ASD. They will be able to process information more efficiently and thoroughly when information delivered in either printed or spoken language is complemented with visual aids. These include pictures, diagrams, charts, graphs, and modeling (deemed an evidenced-based practice; see National Autism Center,

Table 6.1.   An Example of Unpacking an Objective

COMMON CORE STATE STANDARDS	What would students need to do? Lower Order: Remember (knowledge) Understanding (comprehension)	What would students need to do? Higher Order: Apply, Analyze, Synthesize (create), Evaluate,
RI.5.9 Integrate information from several texts on the same topic in order to write or speak about the subject knowledgeably Key Vocabulary: integrate, knowledgeably	Remember: recall information from two or more texts Understand: identify the main idea and supporting detail in two or more texts	Analyze: identify similarities and differences in the information in two or more texts Evaluate: identify information that is relevant and meaningful to speaking knowledgeably about a topic Synthesize: create orally or in writing a synthesis of information from different sources

2011). Google Images and the app Proloquo2go are good sources of pictures.

One of the more effective and widely used types of diagrams is the graphic organizer. Through the shapes and arrows on graphic organizers, the relationship between bits of information can be illustrated. Different text structures, such as cause and effect, main idea and supporting detail, concepts and examples, and temporal sequence of events, lend themselves relatively easily to graphic organizers. There are numerous commercial publications and Internet sources of graphic organizers such as *50 Graphic Organizers for Reading, Writing & More (Grades 4–8)* (Bromley, DeVitis, & Modlo, 1999). If a preprinted graphic organizer is not available, a simple, hand-drawn graphic organizer can often be sketched quickly with information in boxes and lines or arrows showing relationships. For example, a cause-and-effect graphic organizer illustrates the causes for the United States entering World War I.

Tiering a Common Core State Standard

RL.2.4 Describe how words and phrases (e.g., regular beats, alliteration, rhymes, repeated lines) supply rhythm and meaning in a story, poem, or song.

Identify rhyming words or repeated phrases in a story, poem, or song: e.g., while listening to a story, poem, or song containing rhyming words, identify two words that rhyme; e.g., While following along as the teacher reads a familiar poem, identify repeated phrases.

The ubiquity of graphic organizers in learning activities means that they can be added during instruction (with the teacher completing one and presenting it to the class), practice (the students completing either a blank graphic organizer or a partially filled-in one), or product (as a final exercise for demonstrating learning).

When ideas can be physically acted out so the students can see them, they will gain a better understanding. For example, if the class is studying immigration from Ireland to the United States,

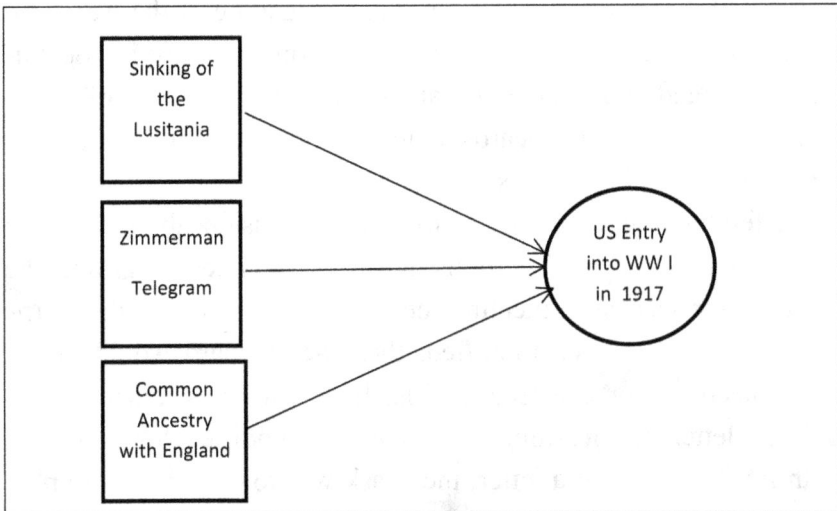

Figure 6.2. Graphic organizer shows causes for U.S. entering WWI.
Source: Peter Griswold

they could produce a skit. A family of students, carrying make-believe possessions, could move from one area of the classroom (labeled Ireland) to another area (labeled the United States), conveying the concept of immigration more effectively for the child with ASD.

Language impairments in children with ASD require special attention to the meanings of vocabulary words that are introduced in lessons. This is an area where teaching and reinforcement is needed so that students with ASD understand the various potential uses of the word. Word meanings can be expanded in multiple ways beyond the dictionary definition: synonyms and antonyms, examples and non-examples, the category the word belongs to, other examples of words in the same category, multiple meanings of the word, and parts of speech are some of the ways that can aid comprehension.

Images and acting out meanings help. Students can be more actively engaged through games like charades, or discussions of their own knowledge of the word (Where have you heard this word? What do you think of when you hear it? Can you use it in a sentence?). In these ways, a deeper understanding of the word and its related concepts are constructed. Additional practice in vocabulary words and their meanings can be arranged through worksheets (crossword puzzles, flashcards, matching exercises) either independently or in learning centers.

Differentiating the product involves a decision about how the student with ASD will demonstrate his or her learning, and the standard for success in meeting the learning objective. If the learning objective has been modified, then the standard would match that objective. For example, in Ms. Everyteacher's lesson on the opinion letter, the learning objective was modified for a student with ASD. Instead of a letter, their task was to complete a graphic organizer with an oval in which they expressed their opinion, and two squares in which they listed the reasons for their opinion.

In other instances, the method for demonstrating learning can be adapted in ways to show that the child is meeting the same learning objective as other students, but the assessment activity is different. For example, the student might take an oral test on a novel, dictate their description of the metamorphosis of a caterpillar into a butterfly, or draw a picture to show how various Native American dwellings reflect the resources in their environments.

In selecting the area(s) to differentiate, two principles should be kept in mind. First, the differentiation should be as minimal as possible, that is, the learning activity should be close to what the rest of the class is doing but still afford the opportunity for success. Second, the differentiation should involve as little of the teacher's time and attention as possible during instructional periods. Following these two principles establishes a hierarchy of interventions.

The first level of intervention is the use of adapted materials and altering teaching styles. For example, a child with ASD may be anxious and overwhelmed by a large number of long-division problems on a page with limited space to write down the calculations. Limiting the number of problems on the page and providing more space to compute the answers takes some extra preparation time, but not class time. Similarly, instruction can be altered with a PowerPoint to help the student process the material.

The second level of intervention involves one-to-one or small group reinforcement following a whole group lesson. This allows the teacher to see where the student is having difficulty, and target supplementary instruction. The disadvantage is that, unless there is a co-teacher or paraprofessional to provide the assistance, the teacher's interaction with the student will, of necessity, be brief.

The third intervention would be to individualize the learning objectives. This is the most substantial of the modifications, since it means that the child will not be held accountable for the same skills and information as the other students. The assumption is that the material is too abstract or there is too much material for the child with ASD to master (see above passage on tiering learning objectives).

Differentiating instruction has been presented, up to this point, as a means of accommodating a child with learning difficulties. In a larger meaning of the word, however, differentiating instruction is a way of designing curriculum, instruction, practice, and assessment for all the learners in the classroom—those below, on, and above grade level. Differentiating instruction can be enhanced through technology. Significant advances in this area have been made through a related teaching/learning method called Universal Design for Learning (Council for Exceptional Children, 2005).

Universal Design for Learning, or UDL, involves creating a classroom with multiple means of representation of content (print, media, oral language), of action and expression (images, print, physical movement, group and individual activity), and engagement (students' curiosity, building motivation). Stein (2013), in a middle school unit on the Civil War, described these multiple means in her classroom: leveled texts, charts, graphs, and illustrations for analysis; teacher lectures, student discussion among themselves, small cooperative learning groups; sketching and highlighting ideas and facts on chart paper, and exploring unknown vocabulary through print and Internet resources (students used their cell phones to access the Internet).

Differentiating report grades is one of the most problematic issues in accommodating students with ASD and is an area best discussed with the school administration to determine policy. It seems unfair to give children with ASD a low grade on an assignment or report card when they are working hard but are unable to perform at the same level as their nondisabled peers. The teacher is not going to feel good about it, after taking the time to tier objectives and adapt instruction and assignments. The parents and the child will, understandably, be upset. What might be suggested are various modified grading systems, which reflect progress and effort:

1. Grade on progress as reflected from pretest to posttest;
2. Target specific content that the child with ASD is expected to master, and assign grades based on that mastery. Allow children with ASD to redo assignments after receiving feedback;
3. Assign different weights to assignments than those used with the rest of the class; and
4. Add points for participation and effort.

BEHAVIOR

For students with ASD, there is the potential for behavior that is different from what is expected of children of their age. This behavior may take different forms. Self-stimulation (such as hand flapping), resistance to directions, and off-topic comments during discussions are common examples. Inappropriate behaviors could be the result of anxious feelings, a lack of awareness of the consequences of actions and expectations for behavior, or unfamiliarity with routines in the classroom.

Regardless of the cause, these behaviors can be initially addressed in the same manner as a teacher would use with other students: a reminder of the rule or procedure and the consequences if the behavior continues. Reminders need to be brief. For example, for the child who touches other children while walking by their desk, "The rule is that we keep our hands to ourselves. If you do it again, we will need to talk about it."

Kaufman et al. (2002) suggests guidelines for speaking with students that seem especially apt for children with ASD:

- Does the teacher have the student's full attention?
- Are the instructions given one at a time, and are they as simple and clear as possible?

- Are the instructions delivered without anger in a clear, firm, but polite tone?
- Has the teacher given the student a reasonable amount of time to comply (keeping in mind that delays in compliance may be the result of the child's difficulty in processing language and connecting it to his/her behavior)?
- Has compliance been monitored?
- Are appropriate consequences administered for noncompliance?

Determining appropriate consequences for children with ASD is a challenge. Typical consequences, such as signs of the teacher's disapproval, withholding a favored treat or activity, keeping a child in from lunch or after school, or sending them to the principal's office, may have little meaning for the child with ASD. On the other hand, what most children would regard as a mild consequence might cause a student with autism great distress; missing a turn at the computer, for example.

In modifying unwanted behaviors, there are several essential guidelines for the general education and co-teacher to follow:

1. Select the behaviors to be extinguished, and make certain that the child is praised when these behaviors don't occur;
2. Identify, describe, and model the behavior that can replace the unwanted behavior;
3. Find the consequences that are meaningful to a child with ASD (often a trial-and-error process that is part of getting to know the child), and prioritize which behaviors are to be addressed first, focusing on those that may impact the safety and learning of the class.

It helps, too, to keep track of the antecedents of inappropriate behavior: keeping records of the time of day, the activity, and proximity of other students.

Is there a single factor that will determine the success or failure of the student with ASD in the general education classroom? Resources, materials, adequate staff, and teaching skills, including the ability to differentiate and individualize instruction, are necessary components of instruction.

However, the most important factor seems to be the teacher's disposition, his or her willingness to accept the student as a member of the classroom. The teacher must be willing to empathize with the frustrations the child experiences, to celebrate the gains, which at times may seem small, and to see others as valued collaborators in shaping instruction. In addition, there will be times when the teacher will need to ask for help and to advocate for programming and resources in order to meet the needs of the child.

Some children with ASD may have a one-to-one aide with them in the general education classroom. Be careful to not fall into the trap of thinking that the paraprofessional will take care of all the child's needs. Monitor the paraprofessional's interactions with the child, and look for opportunities to work with the child. Finally, it is imperative to understand the balance between the roles of teacher and student.

Teachers need to view the inclusion of children with ASD as a partnership in which the child and teacher share responsibility for learning. It is easy to assume a position on one end of the scale or the other. At one end is the teacher who decides that they are going to teach the way they have always taught and it is the child's responsibility to learn. At the other end is the teacher who tries different methods but regards the child as a lump of clay that can be shaped. That view makes the student the passive learner: a vessel into which the teacher pours knowledge, an undefined being, whose conduct is managed by various behavioral strategies.

Teachers have an obligation to teach in ways that foster academic and social-emotional progress; however, the role of the student must not be underestimated. For maximum progress, the student with autism should be an active participant in the process, an independently functioning child with individual traits and preferences who is just as responsible as the teacher for acquiring their education.

SUMMARY

Theory and research underscore the benefits of placement of children with ASD in the general education classroom, but successful inclusion depends upon the teacher's willingness to accommodate the child and to establish high, but reachable standards for participation and behavior. Although there will be learning activities in which the performance of the child with ASD will be consistent with his/her nondisabled classmates, at other times, expectations will need to be individualized.

While the child with ASD presents with a combination of impairments in language, social interactions, and functioning behavior that are specific to the disability, his/her learning and adjustment to the classroom can by enhanced by approaches used with children with other disabilities. These include curricular modifications, adapted materials, varied instructional strategies, and alternate forms of assessment. Graphic organizers, scaffolded teaching and learning, tiered objectives, text enhancements, intensive instruction in word meanings, preparations for changes in routine, and visual aids are helpful.

The Internet and computer programs vastly expand the capacity to provide images that support language-based input. With the assistance of parents and behavior specialists, effective reinforcers can be identified and implemented to shape positive behaviors. Inclusion is successful when collaboration among the teacher, educational specialists, and parents sets appropriate goals, and the teacher possesses a repertoire of strategies to address the needs of the child with ASD.

REFERENCES

Biklen, D., & Burke, J. (2006). Presuming competence. *Equity & Excellence in Education, 39*(2), 166–75. doi:10.1080/10665680500540376.

Chandler-Olcott, K., & Kluth, P. (2009). Why everyone benefits from including students with autism in literacy classrooms. *The Reading Teacher, 62*: 548–57.

Common Core State Standards. (2010). Retrieved from www.corestandards.org.

Council for Exceptional Children. (2005). *Universal design for learning: A guide for teachers and education professionals.* Boston: Pearson.

Daily, M. (2005). Inclusion of students with Autism Spectrum Disorders. New Horizons for Learning. Johns Hopkins University School of Education. Retrieved from http://education.jhu.edu/PD/newhorizons/Exceptional%20 Learners/Autism/Articles/Inclusion%20of%20Students%20with%20Autism %20Spectrum%20Disorders/.

Dynamic Learning Maps. (2015). Center for Educational Testing and Evaluation. Retrieved from http://dynamiclearningmaps.org/content/about-us.

Gill, V. (2005). Challenges faced by teachers working with students with Asperger Syndrome. In M. Prior (Ed.), *Learning and behavior problems in Asperger Syndrome* (pp. 194–211). New York: Guilford Press; cited in Barnhill, G. (2011). Teaching Academic and Functional Skills. In E. A. Boutot & B. S. Myles (Eds.), *Autism spectrum disorders: Foundations, characteristics and effective strategies* (pp. 223–43). Boston: Pearson.

Hardman, M. L., Drew, C. J., & Egan, M. W. (2014). *Human exceptionality: School, community and family,* 11th ed. Belmont, CA: Wadsworth.

IDEA 2004, Title 1/Part B/Section 612 (a)(5).

Kauffman, J. M., Mostert, M. P., Trent, S. C., & Hallahan, D. P. (2002). *Managing classroom behavior: A reflective case-based approach,* 3rd ed. Boston: Pearson.

Kliewer, C., Fitzgerald, L. M., Meyer-Mork, J., Hartman, P., English-Sand, P., & Raschke, D. (2004). Citizenship for all in the literate community: An ethnography of young children with significant disabilities in inclusive early childhood settings. *Harvard Educational Review, 74,* 373–403.

Mastropieri, M. A., & Scruggs, T. E. (2014). *The inclusive classroom: Strategies for effective differentiated instruction,* 5th ed. Boston: Pearson.

McCarney, S. B., & Wunderlich, K. C. (2014). *Pre-referral intervention manual,* 4th ed. Columbia, MO: Hawthorne.

National Autism Center. (2011). Evidence-based practice and autism in the schools. Retrieved from http://www.nationalautismcenter.org/090605-2/.

Ryan, J. R., Hughes, E. M., Katsiyannis, A., McDaniel, M., & Sprinkle, C. (2011). Research-based educational practices with students with autism spectrum disorder. *Teaching Exceptional Children, 43*(3), 56–64.

Simon, D. (2010). *Autism in the classroom: The benefits and drawback of inclusion*. Retrieved from http://www.examiner.com/article/autism-the-classroom-the-benefits-and-drawbacks-of-inclusion.

Stein, E. (2013, May 19). Naturally embedded UDL in no time [web log post]. Retrieved from http://www.middleweb.com/7694/finding-time-for-udl/.

Tomlinson, C. (1999). The differentiated classroom. Responding to the needs of all learners. Alexandria, VA: Association for Supervision and Curriculum Development.

White, S. W., Scahill, L., Klin, A., Koenig, K., & Volkmar, F. R. (2007). Educational placements and service use patterns of individuals with autism spectrum disorders. *Journal of Autism & Development Disorders, 37*, 1403–12.

Chapter Seven

Transition Programs and Practices for Students with ASD/SD

Manina Urgolo Huckvale

In the United States, one important indication of success as an adult is gainful employment. Employment enables us to be self-sufficient, increases our self-esteem, and gives us financial stability (Lindstrom et al., 2011). Finding entry to a career field is one of the top priorities among students ending their education and moving into society. Post-school outcomes for students with disabilities, however, are quite disturbing. The phrase "post-school" is used rather than "postgraduation" for good reason.

A large percentage of students with disabilities leave school with less than ideal education and few marketable skills. Students on the autism spectrum, along with other low-incidence disabilities, are often placed in self-contained classrooms and frequently are not involved with the general school population (Gilson, 2012). By being apart from their typically developing peers, their school days are often lacking in both curriculum and socialization. Most of these students graduate from high school or age out of the school system by their 22nd birthday.

The low rate of high school completion among this group presents several problems, such as higher rates of unemployment and underemployment as well as higher rates of unplanned parenthood and drug use. They leave the system without a transition plan to give them the skills, experiences, and support they need to put them on the road to independence: landing a job and becoming self-sufficient.

While their situation may appear gloomy, research shows that students on the spectrum with low-incidence disabilities can attain employment and lead a quality life, even though they may require outside support. This may be accomplished through a personalized transition plan. This chapter will discuss transition planning as it relates to individuals moving from high school to adult life.

What must we do to ensure that these adults with low-incidence disabilities can transition to stable, long-term employment in a living wage occupation? In other words, how do we build a transition plan? When developing a transition plan, it is important to provide opportunities to develop the skills needed for employment, to gain the experience to develop and hone those skills, and to acquire the support needed to obtain and maintain a job with a livable wage. In addition, these individuals need to develop daily living skills in order to exist as independently as possible.

Research shows that the areas to be addressed in devising a workable transition plan are:

1. A survey of the individual's needs, preferences, and interests
2. Determining an appropriate instruction or Course of Study
3. Identifying related services
4. Finding opportunities for community experiences
5. The development of employment skills
6. Designing post-school living objectives
7. Undertaking functional vocations evaluation. (NJAC 6:A-3.7(d)10i(1-5)

PURPOSE OF TRANSITIONAL PLANNING

Transition planning serves a variety of purposes. It's objective for high school students is to promote a seamless transition to adulthood. It is used to identify specific interventions, resources, and supports required by the individual to achieve desired results. Planning helps the individual develop self-advocacy, decision-making and problem-solving skills to ensure quality outcomes. It promotes social competence and social networking. Furthermore, it provides a career path to high-quality employment and career advancement—real work for real pay! Individuals with disabilities want to be responsible wage earners, not noncontributing members of their communities. This is, of course, "easier said than done!" Let's look at the case of Melissa.

Melissa is a 17-year-old female in the 11th grade with mild intellectual disabilities. She cooperates with teacher/adult instructions, but due in part to some articulation difficulties, she rarely initiates conversations or speaks to her classmates. This has limited her opportunities to make friends and expand her social network.

Melissa's parents are hesitant to let her go out into the community, fearing that she might be "taken advantage of." Melissa's local community does not have public transportation, and she is unable to access other transportation options independently. Her parents are reluctant to help with transportation options due to "safety" issues. Melissa has no job experience outside of what she has acquired through community-based vocational training.

The transition specialist at Melissa's school recently conducted some vocational assessments with her. Melissa completed some interest inventories and researched potential careers. Some of the jobs she is interested in include becoming a child-care worker, a cafeteria cook, a counter attendant, and a mail clerk.

Melissa's transition planning, ideally, should have begun in the elementary grades. The process could have started with showing Melissa a "Dream Sheet," pictures of individuals working at various jobs. She could then have chosen which of these jobs interested her the most. These pictures could have included someone working with children, working in a library, or arranging flowers. Based on Melissa's choice, she could then work with her transition team to explore careers that matched her interests. As Melissa got older, these interests may have changed, so she would have been given the opportunity to revisit her choices from time to time.

How can we help Melissa gain the job experience she desires now, while she is still in school? Her parents refuse to allow her to experience any community-based employment while in school. Therefore, Melissa will not be able to get the experience she needs to become fully employed after high school graduation. This is where the transition team can be helpful in getting Melissa ready for a career after high school.

The transition team can reach out to Melissa's parents and help them understand that developing a life of her own is not impossible, and will not remove her from their lives. With knowledge of all the local resources available to both Melissa and her family, the transition team will be able to help them find solutions to the problems they envision. Once the parents learn that their daughter can move about in the community safely and, through employment, find purpose and pride in her life, they will be able to look forward to a positive future for everyone involved. Often, in difficult situations, the transition team is able to find compromise solutions that satisfy both the child's needs and the parent's concerns.

Transition planning requires a collaborative effort between the school, parents, and community, with instruction in natural settings such as job sites, food markets, and bus stops. These collaborations provide opportunities to develop problem-solving strategies. This planning must involve the student and the teacher, and should involve family members, Child Study team members, and possibly role models such as individuals in the workplace.

The box below suggests websites that provide information to individuals, families, and service providers to help navigate the supports needed to transition from school.

Supports

http://www.StateData.info
http://www.communityinclusion.org
http://www.worksupport.com
http://www.bls.gov/bls/newrels.htm
http://autism.sedl.org
https://www.disability.gov/employment
http://www.ssa.gov/ssi/text-understanding-ssi.htm
http://www.nj.gov/humanservices/ddd/home/index.html
http://lwd.state.nj.us
http://autismnj.org
http://autismnow.org/at-home/learn-and-understand-
    autism/self-advocacy/
http://veryspecialcamps.com/summer-camps/Daisy-
    Recreation-Program-2260.html

SURVEY OF THE INDIVIDUAL'S NEEDS

Once we help Melissa determine her career interests, the transition team will help her develop transition goals. It is important that these goals are attainable, allowing Melissa to gain maximum independence and integration into the community. In addition to determining Melissa's career interests, we also need to ask questions about daily living skills to assess her ability to take care of herself independently. Can she get along with her coworkers (soft skills)? Does she have the skills required for the job itself (hard skills)?

Other questions to consider when developing Melissa's transition plan include whether or not she has any special health-care issues that need to be addressed. Does Melissa have any needs or challenges that would prevent her from working outside her home? Does she have any special training needs? If so, who will provide the education and/or training? What can she accomplish without assistance? What could be accomplished if provided with assistance, such as a job coach, training specialist, or health-care provider? As a teacher, how would you use this checklist in the development of a transition plan?

Autonomy Checklist

Developed by the Youth in Transition Project (1984–1987), University of Washington Division of Adolescent Medicine, and based on a model developed by the Children's Rehabilitation Center at the University of Virginia, this checklist looks at the skills in various settings, including the home, employment, education, and training. It also will provide assessments by grade level and type of disability. The assessments are a checklist that looks at what the student can already do, what skills need practice, when the student plans to start learning this skill, and whether or not the skill has been accomplished.

Examples of the types of skills to assess for the home include the following:

Kitchen

- Operate appliances
- Use common kitchen tools
- Plan and prepare meals
- Follow a recipe
- Put away leftovers
- Set a table
- Wash dishes

Laundry

- Put dirty clothes in hamper

- Sort clothes
- Use washer and dryer
- Iron
- Hand wash
- Fold clothes and put away

Family

- Watch TV with family
- Participate in family decisions
- Take care of pets

Other skills to look for are those dealing with housekeeping, gardening, emergencies, personal skills, health care, community, leisure time, living arrangements, and vocational options.

Source: http://www.iidc.indiana.edu/styles/iidc/defiles/CCLC/transition_matrix/Transition_Matrix.html, downloaded on 6/6/15

INSTRUCTION

Based on Melissa's interests and preferences, her future employment may require more formal education. Instruction may include vocational training programs, apprenticeships, on-the-job training, and postsecondary education such as a two-year or four-year college. It may even mean training for independent living.

MAPS (Making Action Plans)

This person-centered, structured process helps students plan for the future by providing input on their dreams, interests, needs, and fears. The transition team and the student use this input to build trust relationships. Active participation by the student demonstrates a commitment to the plan, while at the same time develops self-advocacy skills.

You are in a class with students who will be working on a transition plan for their upcoming IEP meetings. How would you use MAPS to help determine their career interests?

Sources:

http://pealcenter.org/conferences/2015%20jorgensen %20maps%20for%20school%20to%20adult%20life%20plan ning.pdf, downloaded on 8/19/15.

http://nsttac.org

RELATED SERVICES

Consider the circumstances of a young man named Brian. Brian is an 18-year-old student with moderate intellectual disabilities and corresponding limitations in his adaptive skills. He is enrolled in a self-contained classroom in his local high school. Brian exhibits basic positive social skills and generally gets along with teachers and classroom peers.

Brian has many acquaintances in school, but has very few close friends outside of a few students in his room. He has a tendency to approach and attempt to talk to everyone. Brian lives with a single mother who has kept activities outside of the house limited. Brian enjoys outings with a social club for young adults with disabilities, and participates in local school Special Olympic events.

Brian's mother does not drive, and their community does not have public transportation. Brian has no paid work experience but does participate in his school's job training program. He goes with his class to a large department store, an animal shelter for job training, and he visits other training sites at a supermarket, a home improvement store, and the local library.

Brian's class recently completed a self-directed job search assessment. His results lean toward a career as an animal shelter clerk, a ticket seller/taker, an usher, and a counter attendant in a cafeteria. He enjoys working with animals, but his mother does not believe that Brian could hold a paid position in the future.

Brian's mom wants him to remain in school until he is 21 years old. Mom is expecting Brian to live at home after he graduates. She is dependent on the school system's resources and has always relied on Brian's special education teachers for information and advice. Mom is not currently aware of other community resources that are available, nor is she presently pursuing possibilities for post-school services or activities.

Brian's situation, however, is not without hope. Some private employment agencies contract with businesses to employ persons with disabilities. Other examples of businesses that employ persons with disabilities include a bakery in Georgia (Special Kneads and Treats, Inc.) and a vocational workshop for adults with autism in Asheville, North Carolina (Centering on Children, Inc.).

The Special Kneads bakery was started by the parents of a 24-year-old young man who was about to age out of the Georgia school system. They were worried about what would happen to him when they were gone, so they decided to open a bakery in order to give him a career and a future. Special Kneads now employs nine young adults with disabilities, and is a commercial success.

Centering on Children, Inc. is the creation of a North Carolina therapist who devised simple challenges in problem solving and manual dexterity to aid in his work with children on the autism spectrum. Fellow therapists, seeing the effectiveness of his creations, suggested that he try marketing them. With help from friends, his wife, and two sons, the therapist created "Shoebox Tasks" in the mid-'90s, and has been manufacturing these autism therapy tools ever since. Individuals with autism are employed in assembling and packaging these "tasks."

Unfortunately, such examples of entrepreneurial support for individuals with disabilities are rare. This is not only unfortunate for
those with disabilities, but it also represents missed opportunities
for businesses, small and large, to reap the benefits of hiring work-
ers with disabilities. These benefits include a level of dependability
and loyalty that is rare in the general workforce, as well as other
more tangible benefits including those from government programs
at all levels.

If the student with disabilities has been receiving services in
school, those services may no longer be available once the student
graduates. Some of these services may include occupational and
physical therapy and career training. Transition planning will help
individuals learn how to avail themselves of these services, if still
required after graduation.

Depending on Brian's skills in both the workplace and in the
community, he may require different levels of support. These can
range from job coaches, funded by the Social Security Administration, to one-to-one aides who may help with independent living and
transportation.

The transition plan might include classes on developing self-
advocacy skills, time management skills, and even parenting skills.
While Brian's mother may expect him to live at home after high
school graduation, there will come a time when he may have to live
on his own or semi-independently and he will need those living
skills and supports then.

COMMUNITY EXPERIENCES

Brian's transition plan will also include goals for becoming (or
remaining) a valued member of the community in which he lives
and works. These goals may include places to shop for food and
clothing, where to bank, participation in civic organizations and/or
volunteer programs. He can continue to participate in Special

Olympics, perhaps even becoming a coach to other Olympians. Goals such as these will provide Brian with opportunities to socialize and become a valued member of his community.

DEVELOPMENT OF EMPLOYMENT SKILLS

The transition plan will set goals for employment skills, such as working toward a license in a particular field. If the student is not sure about a career choice, he or she might be encouraged to participate in a career awareness program to explore various community-based work-experience programs.

One goal for both Melissa and Brian would be to meet with a counselor from their state's Division of Vocational Rehabilitation Services to determine what services could be provided after graduation from high school. In developing a plan for employment, Brian and Melisa need to decide whether the employment will be competitive (working for someone else in an integrated setting), supported (competitive, but with ongoing support services for persons with disabilities), unpaid, or military service. Regardless of the type of employment, their transition plans must have goals that will support both of them in the workplace.

POST-SCHOOL LIVING OBJECTIVES

It is important to include goals for adult living. Brian and Melissa may work toward obtaining a driver's license and they will have to plan for insurance needs. Other goals might include registering to vote or opening a bank account. Can Melissa or Brian manage their personal health issues or maintain a home? Can they clean, cook, and shop for groceries? Can they apply for a credit card or manage their debt? Do they belong to the YMCA or a church group? Transition planning should include goals such as these so that any individual with a disability can live as independently as possible.

FAMILY SUPPORT AND EXPECTATIONS

Families should be involved in the development of a transition plan, if at all possible. Family members are among those who know best the skills and abilities of the individual for whom the plan is being written. They can also help assess the individual's abilities in relation to the activities of daily living, both in the home and the community. It may also be possible that the family is not in favor of the student living outside the home upon graduation from high school. However, families need to be aware of the support services available to them and their child in order to take advantage of these resources and prepare for the day that the family is unable to care for that child.

When planning transition goals for students with significant disabilities, it's important that the questions be specific to the student's goals and aspirations, as well as those of the family. In addition, these goals have to be appropriate to the student's level of functioning.

As Melissa's classroom teacher, how would you use the following guiding questions (adapted from Greene & Kochhar-Bryant [2003], "Pathways to successful transition for youth with disabilities") to direct Melissa and her family in developing her transition plan? When planning transition goals for students with significant disabilities, remember to be specific in developing goals that meet the student's goals and aspirations, as well as those of the family. In addition, these goals have to be appropriate to the student's level of functioning.

Guiding questions:

• Can the student express his or her interests? If not, the transition plan must be developed with input from family members and other teachers/caregivers.

- Should any special health-care needs be taken into consideration?
- Are there needs or challenges preventing the student from working outside the home?
- Who will assist the student in obtaining education and/or training for specific jobs?
- What can the student accomplish without assistance?
- What could the student accomplish with professional assistance such as from a job coach or caregiver?

Other questions to ask the student:

- Where do you want to live?
- Where do you want to work?
- Where do you want to learn?
- What do you need to learn now to live where you want?
- What do you need to learn now to have the career you want?
- What do you need to learn now to be able to get that training?

FUNCTIONAL VOCATIONAL EVALUATION

A functional vocational evaluation will develop a vocational profile based on the student's unique individual status. This evaluation will collect information regarding the student's interests and abilities. If completed while in high school, the school and the student can contact agencies within the community to provide job-sampling experiences. Employers can develop a situational employment assessment to determine the student's interest in the employer's field. If the student is successful in a particular employment situation, then goals can be developed to ensure that he or she has the appropriate skills and training in that area.

There are numerous assessment and evaluation tools, but once the student has graduated from high school it becomes more important to have options in place to ensure that the individual will be a contributing member of society. Functional vocational evaluations must revisit basic questions such as: What are the needs or challenges preventing this young adult from working outside the home? What could this person accomplish without assistance? What could this person accomplish if assistance were provided? (Greene & Kochhar-Bryant, 2003).

TECHNOLOGY

We live in a society where just about everyone has at least one high-tech device, such as a cell phone or a radio. Everyone, no matter the level of ability, is expected to have some basic technological knowledge when pursuing postsecondary education or employment. Knowledge of the use of various types of technology provides individuals with greater access to all types of opportunities, especially in education and employment.

When we discuss technology in the workplace, we don't always mean the use of computers but also of other devices that may be available in the workplace, depending on the type of employment. These may be copy machines, postal scales, vacuum cleaners, time clocks, etc. Different types of technology can supplement compensatory strategies to maximize independence in school and in the workplace. Chapter 5 discusses the use of technology in more detail.

COLLABORATION

The important point to remember is that collaboration is key to a successful transition plan. Not only should involvement include the student, teachers, and family members, but the transition team should also include all members of the Child Study team, a representative of the Division of Vocational Rehabilitation, possibly a job coach, and even a school counselor at the high school level. If postsecondary education is in the future, then perhaps a counselor from the disabilities office of the intended college should attend.

Certain practices for transition planning include the implementation of positive behavior supports to address behavior challenges, matching the individual education plan (IEP) with the student's vision for his or her future, taking advantage of inclusive experiences, providing a variety of job and life experiences, and coordinating a smooth transition to living and working in the student's community (Wehman et al., 2009). Since most of these practices are self-explanatory, this author will give just a brief overview of each area:

1. Implementing positive behavior supports for individuals with challenging behaviors will lead to increasing positive communication and social skills needed to succeed in the community and in the workplace. Decreasing inappropriate behaviors will increase the individual's success in work and life experiences. Interventions to implement positive behavior supports were discussed in detail in chapter 4.

2. Matching the school's curriculum to the student's goals for the future will ensure that the student will have the ability to explore career and life goals. Curriculum choice gives the student the ability to decide where he wants to go in life and to focus on pathways for meeting those goals. In order to do this successfully, the student MUST be involved in his IEP and transition development plans. For instance, we know that Brian is interested in working with animals. Perhaps a transition goal for him would be taking a class in tending small animals or volunteering at the local animal shelter.

3. Taking advantage of inclusive experiences by allowing the student with autism spectrum disorder or other severe disability (ASD/SD) to be included in as many activities as his or her peers gives the student a chance to practice social skills in a natural environment with his peers who do not have disabil-

ities. It also gives the student the opportunity to take advantage of the general education curriculum and to observe and learn how to integrate successfully into his workplace and community.

4. The transition plan should include the opportunity to develop work experience to see how tasks are completed and to understand and be able to follow the rules of the workplace. In Melissa's case, she could work in the school cafeteria to see if she really enjoys working in food service. Furthermore, the transition plan should include the opportunity to participate in community activities including, but not limited to, visiting the library, shopping in the local market, and attending or participating in community events. There are different tacit rules for each of these activities, and the student with disabilities needs to understand the rules for each one.

5. Coordinating a transition to living and working in the community necessitates a support system that can enable the individual to make that transition almost seamlessly. This support system can only be successful if the transition team is aware of the student's and family's needs for services. This demonstrates the importance of connecting with various support services while the student is still in school. The student's needs can be identified and properly addressed based on the recommendations of the teachers, Child Study team, family needs, adult service providers, and the student himself. In Brian's situation, for example, learning how to navigate the transportation system will open up opportunities for him both socially and in the workplace.

SUMMARY

Based on these considerations, in writing a transition plan, the student should be able to transition smoothly into either postsecondary education or employment, helping the individual to attain his or her vision for the future and to achieve success beyond school.

Transition planning is a process that should be tied closely to the IEP. Its purpose is to guide a student toward life goals that reflect the individual's interests and abilities. Careful planning will lead to successful outcomes where the individual becomes a productive member of his or her community.

REFERENCES

Gargiulo, R. M. (2015). *Special education in contemporary society: An introduction to exceptionality*, 5th ed. Thousand Oakes, CA: Sage Publications.

Gilson, J. M. (2012). National Association of School Psychologists. Communique 41:1:10. Bethesda, MD.

Greene, G., & Kochhar-Bryant, C. A. (2003). *Pathways to successful transition for youth with disabilities.* Upper Saddle River, NJ: Merrill Prentice Hall.

http://iris.peabody.vanderbilt.edu/cou2/challenge_trans.html, retrieved on December 6, 2010.

Lindstrom, L., Doren, B., Miesch, J. (2011). Waging a living: career development and long-term employment outcomes for young adults with disabilities. *Council for Exceptional Children, 77*(4), 423–34.

NJAC 6A:14-3.7(d)10i(1/5).

Schall, C. (2009). Education and transition planning. In P. Wehman et al., *Autism and the transition to adulthood.* (pp.39–93).

Wehman, P., Datlow Smith, M., & Schall, C. (2009). *Autism and the transition to adulthood: Success beyond the classroom.* Baltimore: Paul H. Brookes, Co.

Index

About the Editors

Manina Urgolo Huckvale, Ed.D., is associate professor and chair of the Department of Special Education and Counseling at William Paterson University in Wayne, New Jersey. Her expertise is in teacher education, special education, and transitions for students with autism spectrum disorders. She is instrumental in building the graduate program for autism spectrum disorders and severe disabilities at William Paterson University. She also has teaching and administrative experience in urban, suburban, and rural communities.

Irene Van Riper, Ed.D., is assistant professor of Special Education in the Department of Special Education and Counseling at William Paterson University in Wayne, New Jersey. Dr. Van Riper is an authority in autism spectrum disorders and is instrumental in building the graduate program for autism spectrum disorders and severe disabilities at William Paterson. She was a reading specialist and a special education teacher for 15 years in Charlotte, North Carolina.

www.ingramcontent.com/pod-product-compliance
Lightning Source LLC
Chambersburg PA
CBHW050442280326
41932CB00013BA/2205